Text by **Toby Musgrave**   *Photographs by* **Clay Perry**

Heirloom Fruits & Vegetables

Foreword by **Raymond Blanc**

With 157 color illustrations

Thames & Hudson

Royal
Horticultural
Society

PHOTOGRAPHER'S NOTE

When we were very young we used to sing a song about a cuckoo in an elm tree. Today's children will not have seen an elm tree and probably not heard a cuckoo. These are just two of the many things that seemed so much part of our lives that have almost completely disappeared. It was towards the end of 2007 that my attention was drawn to a series of newspaper articles stating that due in part to EU bureaucracy we had lost a huge percentage of our traditional vegetable varieties. This news was coupled with stories about orchards being grubbed out and the consequential loss of many ancient fruit varieties.

I felt moved to try to draw attention to the situation and to stop further loss by making a book on the subject. I approached Susannah Charlton and Rae Spencer-Jones at RHS publications, who, with Simon Maughan, were supportive of my idea, and with the help of the Lost Gardens of Heligan I embarked on my project and began taking photographs of endangered fruit and vegetables.

I felt the style of the photography should reflect the traditional nature of the subject, as with my flower photography, which is influenced by the Dutch flower painters. I again looked to the past for inspiration, finding it this time in the shape of the Spanish still-life painters of the 16th and 17th centuries, who have also contributed to the way I approach still-life work, which I see as a series of portraits. Some years ago there was an exhibition of their work at the National Gallery in London and I was deeply impressed by these 300-year-old masterpieces, so perfect in detail and full of atmosphere. I set to work on the fruit and vegetable photographs with these paintings very much in mind, especially the work of Juan Sánchez Cotán, who was a pupil of Blas de Prado, none of whose works survive with certainty to the present. Cotán was born on 25 June 1560, so we share a birthday, albeit some 380 years apart. Much of Cotán's work was painted in a framing space, with which he connected the viewer to the subject by placing objects to the front of the frame, protruding into the space nearest the viewer, creating a sense of depth. The framing device, like a window, was called a Contorero or larder, and it was the custom to hang fruit and vegetables, along with game, on strings in this space to stop them spoiling.

The RHS were pleased with the results of my work and asked Toby Musgrave to write the text. Toby has a tremendous sense of history and knowledge of horticulture, and it is my sincerest hope that this book will go some way to convince people that they should not lose this precious heritage.

Published in Great Britain under the title *Heritage Fruits & Vegetables*.

First published in 2012 in hardcover in the United States of America by Thames & Hudson Inc., 500 Fifth Avenue, New York, New York 10110

thamesandhudsonusa.com

Library of Congress Catalog Card Number 2011935803

ISBN 978-0-500-51618-8

Printed and bound in China by Everbest Printing Co. Ltd

ON THE COVER: *Pea 'Prince Albert'.*
HALF-TITLE: *An autumn abundance of fruit.*
TITLE-PAGE: *Apple 'Nonpareil'.*

SECTION OPENERS
SPRING: *Potato 'Lord Rosebery'.*
SUMMER: *Strawberry 'Royal Sovereign'.*
AUTUMN: *Plum 'Apricot Gage'.*
WINTER: *Broccoli 'Nine Star Perennial'.*

CONTENTS

FOREWORD by Raymond Blanc 7
PREFACE 8
INTRODUCTION: Fruit & Vegetable
Cultivation through the Ages 12

Spring

SPRING VEGETABLES

Asparagus 24
Cauliflower 26
Kohlrabi 30
Potato 32

Summer

SUMMER FRUIT

Apricot 40

CHERRY

Sweet Cherry 42
Acid or Sour Cherry........................... 44

CITRUS

Citron 46
Orange 48
Lemon 52
Lime 54

CURRANTS

Redcurrant & Whitecurrant................. 56
Blackcurrant 58

Gooseberry 60

HOTHOUSE FRUIT

Peach & Nectarine 64
Fig.. 68

Mulberry 70
Raspberry 72
Strawberry 74

SUMMER VEGETABLES

ALLIUMS

Onion 76
Shallot... 80
Garlic 82

BEANS

Broad, English or Fava Bean 84
French or Kidney Bean 88
Scarlet Runner Bean 90

Beetroot... 92
Carrot 94

CUCURBITS

Cucumber 98
Marrow & Courgette......................... 100

Florence Fennel 102
Globe Artichoke & Cardoon............... 104
Pea 106
Radish 110
Rhubarb 112

SALADS

Lettuce 114
Alexanders & Purslane 116

Spinach 118
Tomato... 120

Autumn

AUTUMN FRUIT

Apple... 126
Blackberry 132
Medlar 134

NUTS

Almond 136
Cob Nut & Filbert............................. 138
Sweet Chestnut................................ 140
Walnut 142

Pear 144

PLUM

Common Plum.................................. 150
Damson & Bullace 156
Gage.. 158
Mirabelle 162

Quince 164

AUTUMN VEGETABLES

Celery & Celeriac.............................. 166
Chard 168
Pumpkin & Squash............................ 170

SOLANACEAE

Aubergine or Egg-Plant...................... 174
Chilli & Sweet Pepper........................ 176

Sweet Corn...................................... 178
Turnip 180

Winter

WINTER FRUIT

HOTHOUSE EXOTICS

Grape 186
Muskmelon 190
Pineapple.. 192

WINTER VEGETABLES

BRASSICAS

Broccoli 194
Brussels Sprout 196
Cabbage 198
Kale... 202

Chicory 206
Leek 210
Parsnip 212
Salsify & Scorzonera 214

TUBERS

Jerusalem Artichoke.......................... 216
Tuberous Nasturtium & Oca de Peru... 218

CHRONOLOGY............................... 220
USEFUL ADDRESSES...................... 220
BIBLIOGRAPHY.............................. 221
INDEX 222
ACKNOWLEDGMENTS 224

FOREWORD

RAYMOND BLANC

Chef Patron of Le Manoir aux Quat'Saisons

I still recall vividly how naïve I was when I first came to Britain. I carried no worldly goods with me – only the food culture that was passed on to me by my parents. At a very early age I already knew about the importance of the soil, seasonality and the varieties of fruit and vegetables. The reason: my father had a huge garden, which we had to tend, and its harvest provided for the table, both in summer and winter. The particular variety we grew was very important, as it often defined the ultimate quality of the dish.

So I am passionate about the seasonality and freshness of the produce I use in my kitchens, as I am about giving my guests (and friends and family) ingredients whose – preferably local – provenance I know. These attitudes are widely shared by those who will read this book, and the arguments for them are too well known to need rehearsing here. At Le Manoir aux Quat'Saisons the garden is at the heart of our gastronomy. We are growing 70 different vegetables and more than 300 varieties. A good many of them are heritage varieties.

Each garden is very different, not only in appearance, size and the style preference of the owners, but more importantly in the plant communities within it. Crop diversity is as important as habitat and ecological diversity in ensuring that we have plant adaptation to environmental change, but this value often goes unrecognized. This is why we need such organizations as the Brogdale Collections Trust, curating thousands of historic fruit cultivars, and Garden Organic, with their Heritage Seed Library, now registered as a Plant Heritage national collection. This collection of some 800 vegetable varieties is a participatory programme, inspired not by some dewy romance for past flavours, but because we need to preserve as much genetic diversity as possible – and who better to champion it than gardeners? Where do new cultivars come from if not from the old? Breeders don't have access to drawers full of genes to pick and choose at leisure.

But heritage varieties are also not without flavour. In a recent European collaborative leafy vegetable research programme, several of the collection's 'heritage' lettuces outperformed the commercial standard cultivars in both flavour and disease resistance; and I've found some highly prized and tasty heirloom varieties, which we grow for ourselves. While not many old varieties conform to the standardized stereotypes that some view as 'perfect', equally not all 'New' and 'Improved' introductions live up to their promise either. But every heritage variety of fruit or vegetable comes with a story, and that alone has value. And nuances of flavour cannot be found in standardization.

My own dedication to preserving and, above all, using heritage varieties has led me to plant a new orchard which has a core of historic and heritage British apple and pear trees (along with some historic plums, cherries, berries and even apricots and peaches). In search of the ultimate pear or apple experience, I have cooked with my team hundreds of varieties of fruit: raw, poached, roasted, steamed, baked or puréed. We recorded and noted their history, breeding programme, origin, taste and, as important, their best culinary use.

I hope these pages will inspire you to try a taste of history yourselves and to support those people who are preserving this living, edible heritage.

OPPOSITE *A still life of quince, cabbage, melon and lettuce.*

PREFACE

Do you ever wonder where and when our favourite, everyday fruits and vegetables originated, who first grew them, and how they got their name? And, in particular, which of those grown in the past are still available today? The aim of this book is to reveal some of their stories, to recount their origins and journeys around the globe, to explain how they evolved and developed, and, of course, to introduce you to a range of the surviving heritage varieties that are so beautifully illustrated by Clay Perry's outstanding photography. For the gardener (and seasonally minded cook), the book is arranged into four sections following the seasons, and by echoing nature they are of different lengths. Those concerned with summer and autumn, which yield a cornucopia of fresh fruits and vegetables, are naturally longer than those dealing with the leaner times of winter and spring. Fruits that may be cultivated both within a glasshouse and outside in orchards or against walls are placed in the season in which they ripen outdoors, while fruits grown indoors are found in winter. For though they were cultivated to produce harvests throughout the year, it was such exotic fruits served on the dining table during the winter months that demonstrated a head gardener's skills (and of course also his employer's wealth and taste), and I would like to pay tribute, albeit in a small way, to these remarkable men.

However, at the outset I must offer something of an apology. The second most frustrating aspect of researching this book (of the first, see below) is the paucity of information about those ingenious head gardeners, nurserymen and seedsmen who put so much effort into breeding new cultivars in the past. Along the way we shall meet some individuals for whom cultivars are named, and where at all possible I have told their story. But in many cases the information is scarce or simply nonexistent. On other occasions there is information about the breeder, but their cultivar is now extinct. And so while acknowledging the gaps in the story, I also put out a plea that if anyone reading this has more information about plant breeders and their cultivars I would be delighted to hear from you.

Now, some definitions: what is a cultivar and how does it differ from a variety? To begin with variety. The use of the word in the context of cultivated fruits and vegetables is in fact technically incorrect – variation that leads to a distinct variety of the same species is something that arises in nature as a result of natural selection, and not from interference by man. In the vast majority of cases, what we actually mean when we talk about different varieties of fruits and vegetables are different cultivars. Botanically speaking a cultivar is a plant whose origin or selection is primarily the result of intentional human activity. This is usually because someone has deliberately hybridized plant A with plant B and selected the offspring that displayed the best potential. To be botanically correct, when writing a cultivar name it is necessary to give the genus and species followed by the cultivar epithet. For instance, the familiar King Edward potato is properly *Solanum tuberosum* 'King Edward'. However, in order to avoid unnecessary repetition in the text I most often give just the cultivar name. Another botanical term widely used is 'syn.', which is the abbreviation for synonym, meaning an alternative and now out-dated name for the cultivar. Lastly, for the sake of clarity and simplicity, I use the established and recognized term 'heritage variety' rather than heritage cultivar. The botanical names used throughout are those that the Royal Horticultural Society (RHS, which began life as the Horticultural Society of London in 1804 and became 'Royal' in 1861) recognizes as correct.

All involved in the publication of this book – author, photographer, the RHS and publisher – have been as thorough as possible in trying to ensure that the correct cultivar names are identified and used. However, the sheer antiquity of many heritage fruits and the open-pollination of heritage vegetables can result in some variation. And, as all gardeners know, plants can be mis-named. So if your heritage varieties do not look exactly as in the photographs it may be due to local growing conditions, variety of seed or human error. But if any mistakes do remain, we apologize.

When we come to establishing what constitutes a heritage variety, matters become a little more confused. There is in fact no standard definition. One criterion is that the cultivar is not used in large-scale commercial cultivation and must be propagated by open-pollination in the case of seed or by grafting and cuttings in the case of fruit. Open-pollinated plants are left to the devices of nature for pollination, with the seed they produce generally coming true to type in the subsequent generations. Modern cultivars are often the result of very careful and deliberate breeding under closed conditions, using two particular parents selected for their characteristics. An F1 hybrid is the first generation resulting from such controlled cross pollination, and can only be produced by crossing the same two parents in each generation – seeds from an F1 will therefore not come true if saved. Age is an alternative criterion for heritage status, but there is no set 'cut-off' date: some say a cultivar must be at least 50 years old, others 100. The year 1945 (or 1951) is sometimes arbitrarily used, and some purists say that in order to qualify a cultivar must have been passed down for generations within a family. For the purposes of this book I have taken (with the odd exception) the not-in-commercial-cultivation and propagation definition.

OPPOSITE, CLOCKWISE FROM ABOVE LEFT *Chilli peppers; figs 'Osborn's Prolific', 'Persistent Capri', 'St Ervan', 'Violette de Bordeaux'; tomatoes 'Zapotec' and 'Slankards'; leek 'Lyon'.*

But why all this talk of heritage varieties? Are not nurseries and seed catalogues filled with enough new and enticing fruits and vegetables for us to grow, without dwelling on the past? There are two main reasons why enthusiastic and responsible gardeners are growing heritage varieties. First, to produce fruits and vegetables that possess favourable characteristics absent in many new cultivars or those purchased from commercial growers via the supermarket. Secondly, to make a positive contribution to ensure the long-term survival of what remains of our fruit and vegetable gardening heritage. I stated above that there was an even more frustrating aspect to the research for this book than the paucity of information, and that is how many cultivars have been lost to our generation of gardeners. More accurate would be the words shocking and disturbing. I began by expecting that not all the old cultivars would still be in cultivation. What was shocking was the discovery that Europe has lost perhaps 2,000 cultivars since the 1970s, and in America the Center for Biodiversity and Conservation estimates that 96 per cent of the commercial vegetable cultivars available in 1903 are now extinct.

Such losses are the direct result of a combination of changes in commercial horticultural practices and ill-considered legislation. These changes have been driven in large part by shifts in consumer behaviour and patterns of retail, and so much of the blame lies with us consumers and our love of the convenience of the supermarket and our wish to buy rather than grow our own. As a response, plant breeders have created new cultivars that possess a range of characteristics that our great-grandparents would never have considered necessary: ease of harvest (F1 hybrids all ripen at the same time); robustness to ensure minimal damage during harvest, handling and transport; uniformity of size and shape; longevity of shelf life; and possibly a flavour that will appeal to the broadest range of palates. This is not to say that modern hybrids do not also have advantages and useful qualities, including increased yields and better disease resistance, but they should be developed in parallel with and not at the expense of heritage varieties.

The second driving force behind the losses in Europe began with legislation of the 1960s and 1970s, the effect of which was to make it illegal to sell commercially seeds that were not included on a UK (or other EU country) national list. To list a vegetable cultivar was expensive and only worthwhile if commercially viable – something many heritage ones are not. Thus not only have cultivars been lost, but legal obstacles were put in place that made it more difficult to ensure the long-term survival of those heritage varieties that had survived. Fortunately, some common sense has prevailed as a result of intense lobbying, and the UK government now recognizes a 'Vegetable Conservation Variety', which it defines as 'a landrace or plant variety which has been traditionally grown in particular localities or regions and is threatened by genetic erosion'. There is of course still a cost to list a cultivar, but it is a reduced one.

Perhaps this change of heart came in part from the realization that as well as the regrettable loss of individual cultivars we have also lost significant genetic diversity. One reason why the Irish Potato Famine of the late 1840s was so devastating was that potato cultivation was a monoculture – only one cultivar, 'Lumper', was grown. And when one plant succumbed to the blight so did the entire crop of Ireland. There is a high risk that the same could happen again with monoculture crops grown all over the world – indeed it already has. In America in 1972 several cultivars of sweet corn with similar genetic makeup succumbed to blight: the national loss of the harvest was 15 per cent, and as high as 50 per cent in certain southern states. It is therefore imperative for future diversity that we lose no more cultivars.

Thankfully, some enlightened souls have been alert and made it their mission to conserve and preserve what survived. In the UK, for example, vegetable growers owe a large debt of thanks to Garden Organic (formerly the Henry Doubleday Research Association), which established its Heritage Seed Library in 1979 and today manages a collection of about 800 mainly European cultivars. In America, Seed Savers Exchange, founded in 1975, 'permanently maintain more than 25,000 endangered vegetable varieties, most having been brought to North America by members' ancestors who immigrated from Europe, the Middle East, Asia and other parts of the world'. And just for reference, it is permissible to import seed into the UK from outside the EU.

Heritage fruits enjoy a slightly happier story, due in large part to the Royal Horticultural Society. In 1921 the RHS established its Commercial Fruit Trials at Wisley. In 1952 the collection moved to Brogdale Farm in Kent and came under the control of the then Ministry of Agriculture and Fisheries, and so was born the National Fruit Collection (NFC). The collection currently stands at over 3,500 named apple, pear, plum, cherry, bush fruit, vine and cob nut cultivars.

So where are we now? The commercialization of production and retail has stimulated a wide-ranging debate about what we eat, where it comes from and how it is produced. 'Organic' is now mainstream rather than 'alternative', and one laudable outcome is the renaissance of 'growing your own', with all the additional benefits that entails – a healthy, active lifestyle, eating produce whose provenance and cultivation are known, the preservation of allotments, etc. There is an active movement that conserves what has survived and proselytizes the benefits and delights of cultivating heritage varieties. And we have personal choice. By making ourselves and others aware of the issues, by supporting those institutions that work hard to protect and sustain heritage varieties, by simply growing and eating them and spreading the message, we can all help to preserve what has survived of our heritage while simultaneously enjoying the delicious tastes and rich stories of the past.

OPPOSITE *Beetroots 'Detroit' and 'Cylindra'.*

INTRODUCTION: FRUIT & VEGETABLE CULTIVATION THROUGH THE AGES

Fruit and vegetable cultivation is as old as the advent of civilization itself – that juncture in humankind's evolution when a settled agrarian lifestyle replaced a hunter-gatherer existence. This advance occurred in the Fertile Crescent (roughly stretching from the Levant, through southern Turkey and northern Iraq to Iran) around the 10th millennium BC, and as the ages have passed the range and diversity of cultivated vegetables and fruits both increased and changed. New types were introduced and judicious breeding and selection produced new cultivars, while simultaneously old cultivars were discarded.

From the Garden of Eden to the Romans

To find the earliest evidence of fruit cultivation we must turn to the archaeological record. For instance, a site in the Jordan Valley has recently yielded carbonized remains of fig (*Ficus carica*), thought to be a domesticated form, dating back as far as the 12th millennium BC, possibly predating wheat domestication by around 1,000 years (see p. 68). We also have early literary sources: a Sumerian cuneiform tablet of the mid-4th millennium BC from southern Iraq provides the first documentary evidence of viticulture. Later tablets record the cultivation of fig and pomegranate. A cuneiform tablet in the British Museum gives an account of plants grown in the garden of Marduk-apla-iddina (Merodach-Baladan II), who in 721 BC usurped the Babylonian crown. Among the vegetables are beet (*Beta vulgaris*), cucumber (*Cucumis sativus*), garlic (*Allium sativum*), leek (*Allium porrum*), lettuce (*Lactuca sativa*), onion (*Allium cepa*) and radish (*Raphanus sativus*).

The Old Testament is another early and rich literary source that names some of the vegetables then in cultivation. The Book of Genesis, which may have reached its final form in the 5th century BC, recounts how Noah planted a vineyard and got drunk on his wine (9:20), while Numbers (11:5) mentions the consumption in Egypt of cucumbers, melons (*Cucumis melo*), leeks, onions and garlic. In Deuteronomy (8:8), dating to the 7th century BC, the seven types of produce with which the Land of Israel was blessed are named: wheat, barley, vines (*Vitis vinifera*), figs, pomegranates, olive oil and dates.

In Book VII of *The Odyssey*, attributed to Homer and composed in the 8th century BC, though probably recording details from earlier times, there is a detailed description of the orchard belonging to Alcinous, king of the Phaeacians, which was 'full of beautiful trees – pears, pomegranates, and the most delicious apples. There are luscious figs also, and olives in full growth.' Homer's inclusion of both apples (*Malus domestica*) and pears (*Pyrus communis* subsp. *communis*) is significant: both require propagation by grafting to maintain the desired characteristics of the fruit cultivars.

How Archaic Greeks came to be possessed of the skills of joining rootstock with a scion is unknown, although the technique was also written about by Theophrastus, who succeeded Aristotle as the head of the Lyceum in Athens from 322 BC. He is the author of the first known specifically botanical works: *Historia Plantarum* (Enquiry into Plants) and *De Causis Plantarum* (The Causes of Plants). The former is a description of about 550 species, while the latter is more physiological in its approach. Theophrastus' pioneering works were not only widely read in Classical times, but were also the source of much of the information that Moorish and European writers later incorporated into pharmacopeia and herbals.

In Greek mythology Priapus, the well-endowed god of fertility, was protector of gardens, garden produce and viticulture. In Roman times he shared his portfolio with the husband-and-wife team of Pomona, goddess of garden fruits, and Vertumnus, god of seasons, plant growth, gardens and fruit trees. As the Romans expanded their empire from their Mediterranean homeland, so they took with them as Roman a lifestyle as possible, including wine and food. And it was the Romans, with their conquest of Britain under the emperor Claudius in AD 43, who brought to their northernmost province over 40 new edible plant foods, as revealed by the archaeological record, making what has been described as 'the first serious diversification of the plant component of the British diet since the introduction of wheat and barley in the Neolithic' (see Bibliography).

As early as the 8th century BC, the inhabitants of Britain had cultivated small field plots and there is also evidence for gardens near to houses in which both wild and domesticated plants were tended and grown. Thus the Britons' diet of cereals was supplemented by cultivating and collecting wild-growing vegetables, fruits and nuts. Vegetables included sea kale (*Crambe maritima*), wild celery (*Apium graveolens*), sea beet (*Beta vulgaris* subsp. *maritima*), wild cabbage (*Brassica oleracea*), wild carrot (*Daucus carota*) and wild parsnip (*Pastinaca sativa*). Fruits were more limited: crab apple (*Malus sylvestris*), sloe (*Prunus spinosa*), bullace (*Prunus insititia*), wild cherry, gean or mazzard (*Prunus avium*), wood strawberry (*Fragaria vesca*), red raspberry (*Rubus idaeus*), blackberry (there are several native European species including *Rubus laciniatus*, *R. thrysiger* and *R. nitidioides*) and the hazel or cob nut (*Corylus avellana*).

The Romans imported several foodstuffs for consumption rather than cultivation, including lentil, olive and pomegranate. Some fruits may

OPPOSITE, CLOCKWISE FROM ABOVE LEFT *Gooseberries 'Leveller', 'Black Seedling' and 'Lord Derby'; carrot 'Black Spanish'; 'Iranian Medlar'; potato 'Lumper'.*

ABOVE *A selection from the brassica family: broccoli, cabbage and cauliflower.* OPPOSITE *Grapes: a quintessential fruit of the Classical world.*

have been grown but subsequently died out and had to be reintroduced in medieval times, while others such as apple, grape, black mulberry (*Morus nigra*) and walnut (*Juglans regia*) have remained in cultivation ever since. The same is true of many of the new vegetable arrivals, including leek, lettuce and turnip (*Brassica rapa*). In addition to archaeological remains, the Romans have also left us five texts – four works on agriculture and one encyclopedia – dating from the 2nd century BC to the 1st century AD, which provide a detailed insight into the fruits and vegetables cultivated in Italy and the wider empire: Cato's *De Agri Cultura*, Varro's *Rerum rusticarum libri III*, Columella's *De re rustica*, Palladius' *Opus agriculturae* and Pliny the Elder's 37-book *Naturalis Historia*.

Monks, Monarchs and Nobles

Following the Roman departure from Britain in AD 410 and throughout the so-called Dark Ages it was the monastic houses, with their self-sufficient and ascetic (or supposedly so) lifestyle, that preserved horticultural skills, as well as the individual fruits and vegetables cultivated. Within the confines of monastic gardens, and with the exception of the symbolic Madonna lily and red rose, plants were cultivated for utilitarian purposes – medicinal, culinary, domestic. It was also the literate monks who made the earliest post-Roman records of the plants grown in their gardens and orchards. One of the first is *Capitulare de Villis* (Decrees concerning Towns). Commissioned by the emperor Charlemagne and written around the end of the 8th century by Benedict of Aniane in Languedoc, southern France, *Capitulare* lists 73 herbs and vegetables and 16 fruits. The earliest English source, written in Anglo-Saxon in Winchester between 925 and 940 and possibly commissioned by Alfred the Great, the *Læcboc of Bald*, or Bald's Leechbook, is a healing book. The word *læc*, which can be translated as 'remedies', is also part of the title of another early medicinal work, the *Lacnunga*, which contains nearly 200 treatments and dates to the late 10th or early 11th century. A third source also dates to the 10th century and was penned in Latin by Ælfric, the first Abbot of Eynsham in Oxfordshire. His *Glossary* (*c.* 995) is exactly that, but rather than arranged in an alphabetical list the words are grouped by topic, one of which is plants. It was another two centuries before the first specifically horticultural texts were written in England. Alexander Neckam (1157–1217), a teacher, and from 1213 Abbot of Cirencester, wrote *De Naturis Rerum* (*c.* 1180) and *De Laudibus Divinae Sapientiae* (1213), from which a list of 140 species can be compiled. A further significant source is *De Vegetabilis et Plantis* (*c.* 1260), the work of Albertus Magnus (*c.* 1206–80), a Dominican monk and Count of Bollstädt in what is now Germany. It contains descriptions of 270 species, of which 170 were well known in Europe. Magnus's text is additionally significant in that it provides an early description of a medieval pleasure garden (herber or *viridarium*).

In the years following the Norman conquest of England in 1066, ornamental garden-making thrived as both a royal and a noble pastime. Planting pleasure gardens relied on what was available and many plants

had to multi-task. In the flower beds herbs such as lavender and, from the late 14th century, rosemary jostled with medicinal plants such as peony, clove pink, lesser periwinkle, iris and violet. Fruit was also widely planted ornamentally within the *viridarium* as well being cultivated within the purely productive orchard, the *pomerium*. The horticulturally minded Queen Eleanor of Castile, wife of Edward I of England, not only employed several gardeners from Aragon to tend her new garden at King's Langley in Hertfordshire, but also purchased apple 'Blandurel' for it in 1280. Edward was himself an ardent garden-maker: on his return from the ninth Crusade and coronation in 1274 he took a close interest in the new herbers being laid out at the Tower of London and the Palace of Westminster. Surviving royal accounts from 1277–79 show that a number of different fruits were purchased for the herbers, including three named varieties of pear: rewl, gilefr and 'Kaylewell' (spelt variously as 'Kayl' and 'Kaylew' and probably the same as 'Cailhou'). The last, which had also been planted at the Tower of London in March 1262 by

Henry III, cost 3s 6d each (shillings and pence; throughout this book original prices are given – for those interested in finding out equivalent values today, visit www.measuringworth.com). Almost as expensive were gooseberries (*Ribes uva-crispa*), peaches (*Prunus persica*) and quinces (*Cydonia oblonga*) at 3s each; far less costly were vines at 6s for 600 and cherries at 1s 4d a hundred. Perhaps as Edward proudly walked around his new gardens and admired his fruit trees and bushes he may have recalled his grandfather's somewhat bizarre death. On 19 October 1216 King John died of dysentery brought on by the over-consumption of green peaches washed down with copious volumes of new cider.

John Harvey in his authoritative *Mediaeval Gardens* (1981) estimates that by around AD 800 the total number of plants in cultivation in Britain was in the region of a hundred. Analysis of medieval texts reveals that by *c.* 1400, a millennium after the Romans had left Britain, the number had risen to about 250 – an average introduction rate of one every four years in the preceding six centuries. What is significant is that when English and continental texts are compared it is clear that the contents of gardens and orchards on both sides of the Channel were similar. Moreover, it is evident that the majority of both hardy top (or tree) fruits and soft (bush or berry) fruits, and a goodly proportion of the vegetables with which we are familiar today were in cultivation by the start of the 15th century.

Historians give different dates for the end the Middle Ages, but for the purposes of our story it is 22 August 1485, the day that marked the end of the 30-year-long Wars of the Roses, the death of King Richard III on Bosworth Field and the coronation of Henry Tudor as King Henry VII. His son, Henry VIII, who came to the throne at the tender age of 17 on 24 June 1509 and ruled for the next 37 years, was an avid creator of new gardens. He also had a penchant for fresh fruits and actively sought new cultivars from across the Channel. Henry's passion revived English fruit culture which for a century or so had suffered from neglect and decline. The Black Death of the late 1340s had dramatically reduced the population and the economy had suffered a depression which was particularly marked in rural areas, where orchard cultivation slumped. Moreover, by the mid-16th century many of the fruit types that remained in cultivation were already old fashioned. To acquire new and unusual cultivars the King sent to the Low Countries, while the frequent absence of an *entente cordiale* did not prevent him also buying fruit trees from the French enemy.

Two men in particular were responsible for an influx of new fruit cultivars. Richard Harris, the king's fruiterer, travelled abroad in 1533 and brought back pears, cherries (*Prunus avium* and *P. cerasus*) and apples, including pippin apples (the French *pepin* translates as seedling), which were particularly sought after. With these and others Harris planted a model orchard of 42.5 ha. (105 acres) of land at Teynham in Kent. The second champion was Henry's official horticultural expert, John Wolf (or Jean Le Loup), who from 1538 was granted the substantial annuity for life of 20 marks. It appears Wolf travelled extensively on the continent with the express purpose of acquiring plants for Henry. He is credited with introducing the apricot (*Prunus armeniaca*) from Italy in 1542, and a week before Henry's death in January 1547 was paid £20 for 'trees and sets of sundry kinds out of the realm of France'.

Noblemen also sent abroad for novelty. Sir William Cecil, later Lord Burghley and Secretary of State to both Henry and his daughter Elizabeth I, was one of the foremost garden makers of his age. In 1561 Cecil began to lay out a new garden at Burghley, near Stamford in Lincolnshire (he also owned Cecil House on the Strand in London and Theobalds in Hertfordshire), and in the same year sent his eldest son, Thomas, to Paris under the watchful eye of Sir Thomas Windebank. Windebank also had instructions to obtain unusual plants and fruits, excepting an 'orrege [orange] tree', of which Cecil was already in possession. Accordingly, in April 1562 'a lymmon tree' and two 'myrtles', but not the desired 'pomgranat', were dispatched to Cecil as part of an order being sent to Sir Francis Carew of Beddington Park in Sutton, near London. Carew, also a noted plant collector, is acknowledged as the first person in England to raise an orange from seed – specifically the Seville orange (*Citrus aurantium*), from a pip purportedly received from Sir Walter Raleigh in about 1560.

New Worlds, Strange Fruits

The orange originates from Indochina, and it was the mystic orient, or more specifically the search for sea routes to it, that provided a major stimulus for the 'Age of Discovery'. While the dreamed-of short cut to China would remain just that, voyages took European explorers to the Americas, Africa, India and Asia. As well as returning with riches, ships also brought back exciting new plants. The most significant introductions are members of the family Solanaceae from South America or the Caribbean, which were brought to Europe by the Spanish (or those working for them). These are, of course, the potato (*Solanum tuberosum*), tomato (*Solanum lycopersicum*), sweet pepper and chilli (*Capsicum annuum*), and, although not an edible, tobacco, which among other claims to notoriety became an important pesticide used in 19th-century glasshouses. The potato and tomato were most probably introduced by the Conquistadors, the latter three by Christopher Columbus. Columbus also brought back the French bean (*Phaseolus vulgaris*), scarlet runner bean (*P. coccineus*) and pumpkin (*Cucurbita pepo*).

Another Tudor innovation was the printed gardening book, the first of which, the anonymous *The crafte of graftynge & plantynge of trees*, appeared in 1520, some 44 years after William Caxton had set up his press at Westminster. From this date on the enthusiastic and wealthy

OPPOSITE, CLOCKWISE FROM ABOVE LEFT *Celeriac 'Prinz'; pear 'Bellissime d'Hiver'; broad bean 'Crimson-flowered'; plum 'Apricot Gage'.*

garden owner was presented with a succession of instructional manuals. One of the most popular titles, and the first to discuss the cultivation of both top and soft fruit, was *Five hundred pointes of good husbandrie* (1573) by Thomas Tusser (1524?–80). In addition to the 'how-to' gardening manuals, and in tune with the new age of intellectual inquiry that marked the Renaissance, came the herbals. The first, anonymously authored, was published in London by Richard Banckes in 1525, but the most famous was that by John Gerard (1545–1611/12), *The Herball or generall historie of plantes*, which appeared in 1597. Within its covers the eager reader would discover the first illustrations in an English book of 'Apples of Love' (tomato), 'Battata Virginiana' (potato), 'Ginny or Indian Pepper' (chilli), 'Sisarum Peruvianum' (sweet potato), 'Turkie Corne' or 'Turkie Wheate' (maize/sweet corn, *Zea mays*), 'Madde Apples' (aubergine/egg-plant, *Solanum melongena*) and 'Jerusalem artichoke' (*Helianthus tuberosus*).

As head gardener to that great collector of plants Lord Burghley at his residences in the Strand and Theobalds, Gerard was one of the most respected horticulturists of his day. Nonetheless, 'his' work was not wholly original. For, with the exception of a number of plants that Gerard grew in his own garden in Holborn in London, *The Herball* is a translation of another herbal, *Cruydeboeck*, published in 1554 by the Flemish physician and botanist Rembertus Dodonaeus, or Dodoens (1517–85). Even before Gerard's reworking, this influential tome had been translated into French in 1557 by Carolus Clusius (1526–1609), of tulip fame, and then from Clusius' *Histoire des Plantes* into English by Henry Lyte (1529?–1607) as *A Niewe Herball, or Historie of Plants* (1578). Although for this reason *The Herball* cannot be said to offer an accurate date by which plants had been introduced into England, Gerard's position and reputation did give him the opportunity to collect a huge range of new and unusual plants for his garden. Thus at least as significant as his *Herball* is the catalogue of over a thousand types of plants that he himself cultivated and which he published as *Catalogus arborum, fruticum ac plantarum tam indigenarum, quam exoticarum, in horto Johannis Gerardi, civis et chirurgi Londinenais, nascentium* in 1599. This very rare volume gives a definite date by which

OPPOSITE *Sweet pepper 'Long Red Marconi' (both at the green stage and the riper red).* ABOVE *Pea 'Veitch's Western Express'.*

many exotic plants, both ornamental and edible, were in cultivation in England. Indeed, its date of publication is often erroneously quoted as their introduction date.

Despite many changes in ornamental garden fashions over the next three centuries, one constant was the cultivation of fruits. The early 17th century saw the Cecil family once again in the vanguard. Sir Robert Cecil, 1st Earl of Salisbury, was William's son and his successor as Secretary of State to Elizabeth I and subsequently James I. When James I 'persuaded' his Minister to swap Theobalds for a portfolio of properties, Salisbury set about building a magnificent new house and garden at one of them, the old Tudor manor of Hatfield in Hertfordshire. Salomon de Caus (1576–1626) designed the garden at Hatfield at the same time as he was also working on a new garden for James's wife, Anne of Denmark. Her garden at Somerset House in London became the first in England to incorporate in its design

'a house for orange trees'. Salisbury made the wise decision of appointing John Tradescant the Elder (*c.* 1570–1638) as his head gardener, and desiring a garden filled with rarities dispatched him to Flanders, France and Holland in 1611. The surviving accounts of Tradescant's purchases name some of the cultivars he gathered. A few remain in cultivation, for instance cherries 'Biggareau' and 'Tradescant's Heart', quince 'Portugal', medlar (*Mespilus germanica*) 'Dutch' and grape 'Muscat'.

Unfortunately, the King asked neither Tradescant nor Gerard for advice before he launched into what turned out to be a heroic horticultural failure. One of the 'first appearances' on Gerard's 1599 list was the white mulberry (*Morus alba*). The leaves of this elegant tree, indigenous to central and eastern China, are the preferred food source of the silkworm. Keen to establish a silk industry, James wrote to the Lord Lieutenants of the English counties in 1607–08 instructing them to plant mulberry trees.

As many as 100,000 were planted, but the King had mistakenly ordered the planting of the black mulberry upon which the silkworm will not feast.

With the Restoration of the monarchy in 1660 fruit cultivation became an even more fashionable pursuit among the wealthy. The grape, cucumber and melon were all the subjects for much debate and advice, in particular their cultivation within the protected environment of the glasshouse. Also requiring to be cultivated in a specially designed form of greenhouse, and causing as much if not more excitement as any new exotic floral treasures, *the* fashionable fruit to cultivate arrived in 1688, not from its native South America but via Holland. This prickly, tricksy character was the pineapple (*Ananas comosus*), and in 1689 the first English-grown fruit was presented to Queen Mary II. The Queen was an avid collector of hothouse plants, having brought her collection of 400 exotics from Holland. In so doing Mary gave glasshouse design a boost, introducing the sloping glass façade, which made its debut in the three hothouses, each 16.76 m (55 ft) long, erected in the Pond Yard (renamed the Glass Case Garden) at Hampton Court palace.

Innovations and Advances

Constant innovation pushed glasshouse design forwards as fast as technology allowed, and horticultural advances ensured that the maximum benefit was gained from such protective structures. Indeed, the contribution of the greenhouse to the cultivation of fruits and vegetables in the 18th and 19th centuries cannot be overestimated. By the second half of the 18th century a range of heated glasshouses, hothouses and stoves, now constructed with glass roofs and end walls supported by a wooden framework, as well as hotbeds, frames and pits, were an essential component of any self-respecting country estate. For the benefit of the occupants, the lean-to structures were erected within the protection of walled kitchen gardens with the rear brick wall whitewashed. The brick absorbed heat throughout the day and released it at night, while the whitewash reflected incoming sunlight back into the glasshouse. Specific structures were designed for specific crops, and named accordingly. The words 'vinery' and 'pinery' were coined by Thomas Mawe and John Abercrombie and entered the language in 1788 in the 12th edition of their hugely popular *Every Man his own Gardener* (first published in 1767). Much cultural emphasis and experimentation were now placed on 'forcing' – extending the harvest season of as wide a range of edibles as possible by bringing it forwards in spring and prolonging it into winter using heat and protection. Thus fruits were joined in glasshouses by numerous vegetables – potatoes, beans, salads, tomatoes, cucumbers, etc, which otherwise would naturally find their home in the 'open ground'.

Such skilled gardening activities reached their zenith in the years before the First World War as the literally thousands of head gardeners experimented and innovated in 'their' gardens. Every imaginable cul-

tural and cultivation technique underwent extensive test and trial, and improvements were compounded by advances in the sciences of horticulture. One area of notable endeavour was plant breeding, and if the range of different types of fruits and vegetables in cultivation did not increase markedly, the numbers of individual cultivars most certainly did. Fruit breeding was the realm of head gardeners and specialist nurseries, vegetable breeding predominantly that of seedsmen – including some familiar names. Sutton's Seeds began life as House of Sutton in 1806 and Thompson and Morgan was established in 1855.

To put the advances in some perspective, George Bliss described 121 apple cultivars (81 per cent of which remain in cultivation) in his *The Fruit Grower's Instructor* (1825), a number which rose to 253 by the 5th edition of Robert Hogg's *The Fruit Manual* (1884). A comparison between Sutton's seed catalogues of 1852 and 1899 reveals that, for example, the number of asparagus cultivars offered rose from one to five, broad beans from 14 to 16, cucumbers 21 to 28, and peas 53 to 79. What is equally revealing is that the catalogues demonstrate that vegetable cultivar loss was also occurring – the same happened with annual seed cultivars, so popular for bedding displays. A comparison of names reveals a high level of disappearance as new cultivars superseded their predecessors. By 1899 all Sutton's asparagus were new, and only six broad beans, three cucumber and three peas were still available from those listed in 1852. Moreover, the majority of the cultivar names were prefixed by 'Sutton's', indicative of an extensive and successful breeding and selection programme in order to bring new cultivars to the gardener.

Sadly, the powerhouses of horticultural innovation, the great country house gardens of Great Britain, with their extensive kitchen gardens, were one of the victims of the upheavals of the First World War. In its aftermath neither the labour nor the finances were available to maintain pre-1914 standards. And so the major loss of cultivars so long in cultivation began. Yet we gardeners of today should be proud and optimistic, for we are continuing a long and rich tradition of growing fruits and vegetables that extends back some 10,000 years. We have a wealth of literary sources available, both historical and current, which can advise us on best cultural practices. And we have the resources that allow us to choose which fruits and vegetables to grow (many established seed companies are now also offering heritage varieties alongside their modern cultivars). Personally, I find there are many good reasons for choosing heritage varieties: some I have already outlined, but an additional one has nothing at all to do with the act of gardening. It has to do with the pleasure and interest I derive from the stories, literally the heritage, associated with heritage varieties. For me, planting and growing a small bit of history is every bit as rewarding as nurturing, harvesting and eating it.

OPPOSITE *Apples 'Harvey', 'Bess Poole', 'Annie Elizabeth' (in basket) and 'Golden Russet'.*

Spring

Every season has its particular scents: those of spring are the rich, dark chocolate aroma of freshly dug soil and the verdant crispness of new shoots. And the mood of every season is emphasized by its light. Spring light is gentle and comforting, highlighting the fresh greens of developing growth and hinting at excitements to come. This is a time of anticipation and waiting, for deliveries of seed packets full of promise, for the soil to dry out and warm up, and for the mornings and evenings to stretch out, in order to begin the gardening year. Soon it seems there is not enough time to do everything – to dig, till, sow, transplant and prune – to ensure a successful season in the kitchen garden. But it is good also to pause, to revel in the annual marvel of seeing seeds germinate and to take pleasure from nurturing plants and watching them grow.

The first shootes or heads of Asparagus are a Sallet of as much esteeme
with all sorts of persons, as any other whatsoever, being boyled tender,
and eaten with butter, vinegar, and pepper, or oyle and vinegar,
or as every ones manner doth please.

Parkinson, 1629

SPRING VEGETABLES

ASPARAGUS
Asparagus officinalis

Asparagus is a herbaceous perennial native to North Africa, western Asia and most of Europe; the-low growing or prostrate British native found in coastal locations is the subspecies, *Asparagus officinalis* subsp. *prostratus*. In ancient Egypt asparagus was presented as an offering to the gods, and although the Greek authors Theophrastus and, later, Dioscorides, do not mention its cultivation they do refer to a wild *asparagos*. The distinction between wild and cultivated garden asparagus was made by Cato (epicureans preferred the wild form, known as *corruda*), though the difference is only a linguistic one as both are genetically the same. Cato's detailed advice on cultivation given in the 2nd century BC is almost exactly the same as that offered today, and asparagus seems to have been an especially popular Roman vegetable. Pliny also discusses its cultivation at length, and instructions for cooking it appear in Book III of *De Re Coquinaria* (On the Subject of Cooking), a famous Roman collection of recipes dating to the late 4th or early 5th century AD, pseudepigraphically attributed to the gourmet Marcus Gavius Apicius, who lived some time in the 1st century AD.

Archaeological evidence reveals that Romans grew asparagus in Britain and it seems likely that they introduced the upright, cultivated form. Asparagus is mentioned in the *Lacnunga*, where its Old English name is given as *eorthnafele*, and the literary evidence (or lack of it) may indicate that asparagus fell from cultivation and was subsequently re-introduced. The next reference is in *The Names of Herbes* (1548) by William Turner (?1508–68), who gives 'Sperage' as one name for it, and from this date on asparagus became increasingly popular once again. Asparagus (and cauliflower, see p. 27) achieved fashionable status in 17th-century France,

being a particular favourite of the Sun King, Louis XIV – he had glasshouses constructed to produce an all-year-round crop. With such a royal seal of approval, added to the fact that French cuisine was becoming all the rage, asparagus grew in popularity in England too.

By 1670 Leonard Meager (*c.* 1624–*c.* 1704) in *The English Gardener* states that London was well supplied with forced asparagus raised on hotbeds, though early in the 18th century complaints were made that asparagus grown on night soil from London's privies was of 'a Colour unnatural, and a Taste so strong and unsavoury'. The technique of hotbed cultivation was still in use in the 19th century, when a forced crop could be harvested from November through the winter months until outdoor raised asparagus was ready for spring cutting. Nowadays, perhaps because it requires three to four years of patience between planting the crowns and taking the first cut, growing asparagus has declined in popularity. For those wishing to try, asparagus, with its fern-like foliage that turns a lemon yellow in autumn, is also an attractive addition to the ornamental garden.

Asparagus was grown in North America from the 17th century, and one heritage variety still available and of American origin is 'Connover's Colossal'. Bred by S. B. Connover of West Washington Market, New York, and renowned for its very large spears, this was in cultivation by 1866. Another heritage variety that can be grown is 'Mary Washington', bred by Dr J. B. Norton of the US Department of Agriculture in the early 1900s.

OPPOSITE *Asparagus 'Connover's Colossal'.*

The [cauliflower] hath a much pleasanter taste than eyther the Coleworte or Cabbage of any kinde, and is therefore of the more regard and respect at good mens tables.

Parkinson, 1629

CAULIFLOWER
Brassica oleracea Botrytis Group

The cauliflower is a form of the wild cabbage (*Brassica oleracea*) that has been selectively bred for its large white curd formed of what are botanically described as 'aborted floral meristems'. It seems to have been unknown to both Classical and medieval writers, and the first northern European reference appears in Clusius's *Histoire des plantes* (1557). However, the first overall European reference, dating to around 1080, comes from Moorish Spain and is found in the famous agricultural treatise, *Diwan al-filaha*, written by Ibn Bassal, a botanist based in Toledo, in which he describes three types. The date and source of this reference suggest that the cauliflower is of Mediterranean origin, which is supported by later authors, who in fact offer a possible location. In his *Historia generalis plantarum* (1586), the French author Jacques Daléchamps specifies Cyprus, giving one French name as 'Chou de Cypre'. The cauliflower was first recorded for sale in London markets in 1619, and in the edition of his herbal published in the same year Henry Lyte calls it 'Cypress coleworts'. The name, 'Coley flowers', given by Gerard in his 1599 list of garden plants means 'flowering cole' (or colewort, the medieval name for brassicas), and this is an alternative derivation to the oft-quoted Latin *caulis* and *floris* meaning 'flowering stalk'.

The cultivated cauliflower was, however, encountered earlier and further south by the German physician and botanist Leonhard Rauwolf. He travelled through the Middle East between 1573 and 1575 and found the 'Cauliflore' growing at Aleppo in Syria. And Prosper Alpinus in his work *De Plantis Aegypti* (1591) notes that the only brassicas he encountered in Egypt were the cauliflower and kohlrabi (see p. 30). Yet how the cauliflower reached northern Europe from either Spain, Cyprus or the Middle East, and why it took 400 years, remain mysteries. Also perhaps curious and intriguing is the fact that at a time in the 16th century when the cauliflower was still relatively uncommon in Europe it was, accord-

ing to Girolamo Benzoni in his *Historia del Mondo Nuovo* (History of the New World, 1565), flourishing in the New World on the island of 'Hayti' (Haiti), where it had been taken by the Spanish.

The last of the great herbalists, and apothecary to King James I, John Parkinson (1567–1650) was an enthusiastic supporter of the 'Cole flower' in his famous *Paradisi in Sole Paradisus Terrestris* (Park-in-Sun's Terrestrial Paradise, 1629). A century after Parkinson's endorsement, and having become a royal favourite of Louis XIV, along with asparagus, Philip Miller (1691–1771) in his *The Gardeners Dictionary* (1731) gives over five pages of cultivation advice to the 'colliflora', revealing that the cauliflower had become very popular. Half-a-century later again in the 9th edition of *Every Man his own Gardener* (1782) Mawe lists two types – early and late.

Sadly, none of the very early cultivars has survived, but 19th-century heritage varieties that are still available include 'Purple Cape', which was introduced to Britain *c.* 1808 by Marmaduke Dawnay and has a 'close, compact head, of a purple colour' that turns green when cooked, and 'Dwarf Efurt', popularly known as 'Snowball' (1830), which has heads that 'possess the peculiar white, curdy character so rarely attained'. 'Autumn Giant' (by 1838) is described as having heads that 'are very large, beautifully white, firm & compact, & being well protected by foliage, remain a long time fit for use'.

An unusual cauliflower that has become popular in the past decade or so is the rediscovered Italian cultivar 'Romanesco Minaret', which has a flavour somewhere between cauliflower and broccoli and is often misnamed a broccoli. This very beautiful vegetable (it is almost too pretty to eat) is an example of the spectacular fractal patterning that can appear in nature.

OPPOSITE *Cauliflower 'Snowball'*. OVERLEAF *Cauliflower 'Romanesco'*.

The Corinthian turnip grows to a very large size,
and the root is all but out of the ground.

Pliny, 1st century AD

KOHLRABI

Brassica oleracea Gongylodes Group

Kohlrabi is another form of the wild cabbage, and the name literally means 'cabbage turnip' – 'kohl' being the German for the former and 'rabi' the Swiss-German word for the latter. Although it somewhat resembles the turnip, the kohlrabi has been selected for its lateral meristem growth, so that what is eaten is in fact a swollen stem rather than a swollen root. Some authorities claim that the kohlrabi was cultivated during the reign of Charlemagne and appears as *ravacaulos* in *Capitulare de Villis*, but it is not named in any other medieval source. Others say that kohlrabi has a more ancient pedigree and that the Romans grew it, quoting Pliny's description of a 'Corinthian turnip' and a reference in Apicius, but again the evidence is not conclusive and there is much confusion as to exactly which vegetable various sources are referring to when discussing such things as 'turnip-cabbage', the 'turnip-rooted cabbage' and rutabaga, among others.

The first substantiated account of kohlrabi was by the Italian Pietro Andrea Gregorio Mattioli (Matthiolus), who in his *Commentarii, in Sex Libros Pedacii Dioscorides* (1554) states that the kohlrabi had lately come into Germany from Italy. Two decades later, Rauwolf encountered it in the gardens of Tripoli and Aleppo, and in 1591 Alpinus recounts its cultivation in Egypt. Taken together with the evidence concerning other forms of wild cabbage – broccoli (see p. 194), Brussels sprout (see p. 196), cabbage (see p. 198), kale (see p. 202) and cauliflower (see p. 26), it would seem that the domestication and development of kohlrabi and cauliflower occurred at the same time. If so, they both share a common origin somewhere in western North Africa or the Middle East and are more recently domesticated forms of *Brassica oleracea* than their near relatives.

For some reason, kohlrabi has never enjoyed much popularity in Britain. Gerard (1597), the first English author to mention it, says it 'groweth in Italy, Spain and Germany', from where it arrived in England. John Claudius Loudon, in the 3rd edition of his *An Encyclopaedia of Gardening* (1825), makes the rather odd observation that until recently kohlrabi was the only vegetable grown in Poland. However, kohlrabi was sold by the seedsman John Kernan in 1849, and two cultivars – 'Early Green' and 'Early Purple' – were offered by Suttons in 1879. By 1899 these had been renamed 'Earliest Green' and 'Earliest Purple', and in that same year Webbs listed 'Early Vienna' and 'Early Purple'. It is likely that these are the heritage varieties still available today: 'Purple Vienna' and 'White Vienna' (syn. 'Green Vienna'), the latter especially noted for its delicate flavour.

OPPOSITE *Kohlrabi 'White Vienna'.*

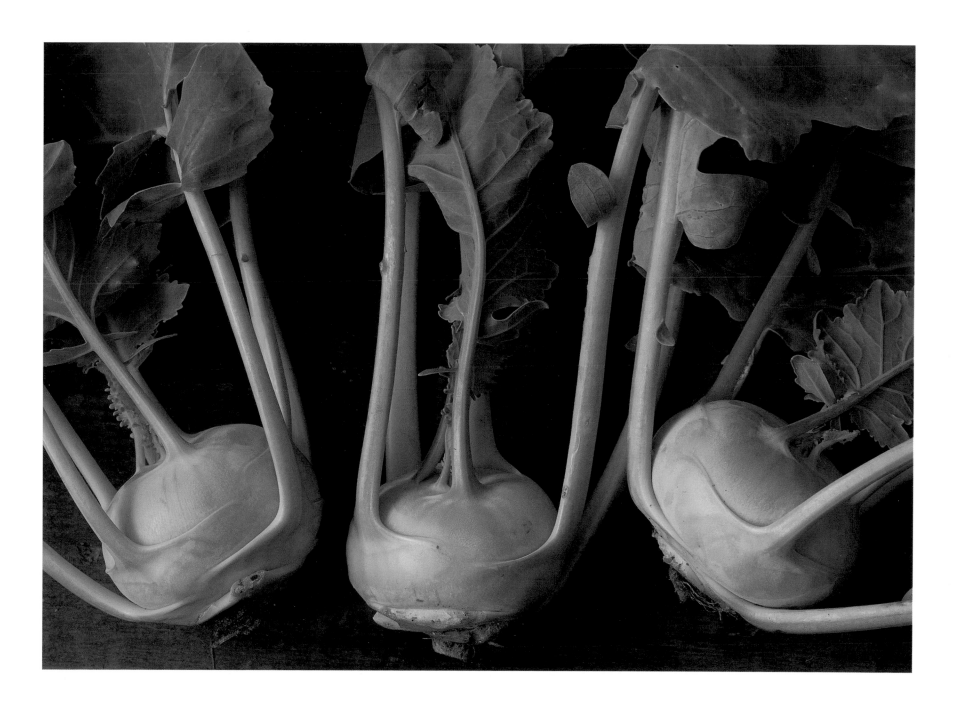

POTATO
Solanum tuberosum

The humble potato (spud, tater or tattie) is a most useful tuber. It is highly nutritious – 0.4 ha (1 acre) will sustain 10 people for a year – and very versatile, thriving in challenging growing conditions that include high latitudes, high altitudes and poor soil. A New World vegetable, the potato belongs to that diverse and useful family, Solanaceae, whose members also include the tomato, aubergine, Cape gooseberry, peppers and chillies, as well as tobacco and deadly nightshade. It is indigenous to the Andes, where eight (possibly nine) species grow wild and are the progenitors of the 3,000 or so varieties and cultivars now in existence. And it was in the high Andes of southern Peru that the process of domestication and plant breeding began some 5,000 years ago.

The English word potato comes from the Spanish for the tuber, *patata*, and the Spanish Royal Academy informs us that this is a compound of the Taíno word *batata* for sweet potato and the Quechua word *papa* for potato. Indeed, 'potato' originally referred to the sweet potato, an etymology that has confused the history of the potato's introduction to Europe. However, as can best be determined, Spanish Conquistadors first encountered the potato in 1534, and three years later Juan de Castellanos described what he called 'truffles' as 'of good flavour, a gift very acceptable to Indians and a dainty dish even for Spaniards'. The potato was taken east from South America to the Canary Islands in *c.* 1562, and from there made the journey to Antwerp five years later. It arrived in Spain in 1565 at the hands of the explorer Gonzalo Jiminez de Quesada. By 1601 Clusius records that the potato was in common use in northern Italy for animal fodder and human consumption – in that order.

Exactly when the potato arrived in Britain, and who brought it, remain a matter of debate and legend, although it does seem that it was a distinct introduction from South America rather than acquisition via Europe. Contrary to popular myth, the 'potatoes' brought back in 1564 from 'the coast of Guinea and the Indies of Nova Hispania' by the English slave trader John Hawkins were in fact sweet potatoes. The other main claimant to the title of introducer is Sir Walter Raleigh, who allegedly planted them on his estate at Myrtle Grove near Cork in Ireland in 1589 and then presented tubers to Elizabeth I. Yet, already in 1569 Mary,

Queen of Scots had complained that the garden at Tutbury Castle in Staffordshire where she was held prisoner was 'a potato patch … fitter to keep pigs in'.

The earliest English depiction and description of the potato is provided by Gerard in his *Herball* (1597), in which he called it the 'Virginian potato'; he is even shown on the frontispiece of the book with a spray of potato flowers. By 1599 Gerard was cultivating both the 'bastard potato' (the potato) and the 'Spanish potato' (sweet potato) in his own garden. Early in the 17th century the potato seems to have been considered a delicacy, since royal accounts for 1619 show potatoes were supplied to the household of Queen Anne, wife of James I, at the then substantial cost of 1s per pound.

From the mid-17th century onwards as the potato became more widely cultivated and affordable it was promoted in England and Europe as a crop to prevent famine among the poor. It seems, however, that the poor were not so easily convinced. One reason that it took time for the potato to become accepted was because its stems, leaves and green tubers are poisonous if eaten. Thus the potato came to be regarded as an evil plant, accused of causing sterility, syphilis, scrofula and leprosy. Some even considered it the 'forbidden fruit' of the Garden in Eden. The Puritans objected to it because it was not mentioned in the Bible; others were more straightforward in their prejudice and considered it fit only for the poor – though they would not eat it. In Britain, according to Charles M'Intosh in his *The Book of the Garden* (1855), discrimination against the potato continued well into the 18th century, particularly in Scotland, where potatoes were a rarity until the 1740s.

One enlightened soul was Lieutenant James Cook, who took tubers with him on his first circumnavigation of the globe in 1768 as part of his policy to plant market gardens wherever he landed as a source of food for future expeditions. Slowly, the potato and its cultivation became more

OPPOSITE: ABOVE *Potatoes 'Snowdrop' (on scales), 'King Edward' (top left), 'Ryecroft Purple' (front left) and 'Edzell Blue' (front right);* BELOW LEFT *potato 'Salad Blue';* BELOW RIGHT *potato 'Edgecote Purple'.*

ABOVE *Potatoes 'Salad Blue', 'Ratte' and 'Vitelotte' (left to right).*

ABOVE *Potatoes 'Lord Rosebery', 'International Kidney' and 'Herd Laddie' (left to right).*

widespread and accepted. Perhaps the most cunning ruse to promote its popularity was employed by the Frenchman Antoine Augustine Parmentier in the 1780s. Relying on human inquisitiveness and acquisitiveness he planted potato fields on the outskirts of Paris in areas inhabited by the poor and placed a guard on them. Local interest was aroused – anything worth guarding must be worth stealing – and one night when the guard 'forgot to turn up' the potatoes were 'acquired' and subsequently grown. The potato even gained a royal seal of approval and set a fashion when Louis XVI pinned potato blossom to the curls of Marie Antoinette, so setting a fad for ladies of the court to follow.

> It was but little cultivated till of late;
> these Roots being despised by the rich,
> and deemed only proper Food for the
> meaner sort of Persons; however, they are
> now esteemed by most People.
>
> Miller, 1754

The one country where the potato was immediately and enthusiastically taken up was Ireland, and by the 17th century its consumption there exceeded that of every other food, fuelling a population increase. But this population was to be devastated by one of the greatest tragedies in recent history. By the mid-19th century the only cultivar grown was 'Lumper'; named for its knobbly shape, it was introduced in 1810 by a farmer in the southwest of Ireland. However, as it turned out it was particularly susceptible to potato blight (caused by the fungus *Phytophthora infestans*). The subsequent crop failure led to the Potato Famine, which ravaged Ireland between 1845 and 1849 and reduced the population by more than half through death and emigration.

In the aftermath of the famine one of the main aims of potato breeders was to produce a blight-resistant cultivar. A leading exponent was Robert Fenn, a retired head gardener, who developed many new cultivars including 'International Kidney' (1879), now better known as 'Jersey Royal', which is a First Early potato. In the 19th century potatoes were, and still are, classified into one of three groups depending on time from planting to harvest: First Early (10 weeks to harvest); Second Early (13 weeks); and Maincrop (20 weeks). To extend the season, potatoes were routinely forced in a glasshouse and grown in pots, 'beds of fermenting material' or 'tanked pits' to ensure an all-year-round harvest.

Thankfully, many heritage varieties of potato remain available and several have interesting stories attached to them. The First Early 'Myatt's Ashleaf Kidney' produces kidney-shaped tubers with light-buff skin and yellow floury flesh. It was developed at the Manor House in the village of Adlington in the Vale of Evesham by an anonymous gardener to Arthur H. Savory. As recounted in Savory's *Grain and Chaff from an English Manor* (1920), this 'methodical old man … at one time had made a hobby of raising new kinds of potatoes'. His finest creation was this cultivar, which he sold to a Mr Myatt for a guinea, and who named the potato for himself. Bred specifically to add appropriate colour to a meal served to the Duke of Burgundy at the Savoy Hotel in London, the Maincrop 'Highland Burgundy Red' dates to 1936. The tubers are oval and the flesh is mostly burgundy red, with a definite ring of white just beneath the skin – it makes excellent novelty chips, crisps and mash. Introduced in 1915, 'Edzell Blue' is a Second Early that produces small, round, blue- or purple-skinned tubers with contrasting tasty white flesh. Another purple-skinned, white-fleshed potato is 'Ryecroft Purple', a Maincrop that predates 1920; it has good blight resistance but is not high yielding. Other Maincrops include 'Snowdrop', with white skin and flesh; 'Flowerball', which dates to 1895; and the perennially popular 'King Edward', which was introduced in 1902 by John Butler.

Legend has it that 'Shetland Black', from the islands of that name, can trace its origin to 1588 and a wrecked and looted ship of the Spanish Armada. However, there is no firm evidence of its existence before 1923. Its purple-black skin has a lovely hue but can be tough, while the flesh is white, mottled with purple and both floury and dry. With a high blight resistance when grown organically, 'Edgecote Purple' was first listed in 1916 and has long oval tubers with yellow flesh and a firm waxy texture; it is, apparently, very popular in high-class restaurants. Dating to 1872, 'Salad Blue' is a Maincrop with distinctive intensely blue-black skin. The pigmentation is also found in the flesh, which is fluffy and disintegrates on boiling, though it does retain its colouring, making it perfect for unusual mash and chips. Also a Maincrop is 'Ratte' (syn. 'La Ratte', 'Ratte de Touquet' and 'Asparges'), which originated in either France or Denmark and is favoured for its distinctive, nutty flavour and smooth, buttery texture. An unusual cultivar with almost black skin and blue-violet flesh, 'Vitelotte' (syn. 'Négresse' and 'Truffe de Chine') is a French cultivar from the early 1800s and is believed to have been introduced from Bolivia or Peru.

And what of the chip? Thomas Jefferson is rumoured to have served chips, or fries, at Monticello, Virginia, as early as 1802, but expert opinion is divided as to whether the French or Belgians can claim the invention. What is fact is that chips became 'fast food' simultaneously on both sides of the Atlantic in the 1860s when cheap cooking oil became widely available for the first time.

OPPOSITE *Potatoes 'King Edward' (top left), 'Snowdrop' (in bowl), 'Flowerball' (front left) and 'Edzell Blue' (front right).*

Summer

Summer's scent is fervent, urgent and vital – it is the sweetness of freshly mown grass, the particular smell of rain on hot dry soil and the heady tang of ripe tomatoes in the greenhouse. This intensity is matched by the light. Strong sunshine highlights the deep shades of green vegetation and skies the blue of a kingfisher's wing. The kitchen garden is now reaching a peak. It is a season to enjoy the bounties of nature, but also a time of vigilance and anxiety, as the weather and pests can threaten delicate crops before they are ready. Most important, however, is to take a moment between the hectic activities of weeding, watering, staking, picking, podding, shelling and peeling, to reflect, to assess what has been successful, and what has not, and to enjoy the satisfaction of a job well done – so far.

Dr Grant hardly knows what the natural taste of our apricot is … for it
is so valuable a fruit; … and ours is such a remarkably large,
fair sort, that what with early tarts and preserves,
my cook contrives to get them all.

Austen, 1814

SUMMER FRUITS

APRICOT
Prunus armeniaca

The apricot – the name is derived from the Latin *praecoquum* for 'early', because it ripens before the peach – is a member of the family Rosaceae and is thus related to a number of other significant tree fruit, including apple and quince, as well as several popular soft fruits such as blackberry, raspberry and strawberry. More closely related still are the other members of the genus *Prunus* – cherry, peach, pear, plum and almond; all are what is botanically termed a drupe fruit, which is composed of three layers surrounding the seed. When we eat an apricot, cherry, peach, pear or plum – but not an almond (see p. 136) – we consume the skin, or exocarp, and the flesh, or mesocarp, and we discard the hard pit or stone, the endocarp, inside which is the seed.

The apricot is native to northeastern China (not, as its species name would suggest, Armenia), where it may have been cultivated for 4,000 years and was believed to be beneficial to female fertility. With its rich, warm colours, intense perfume, luxuriously sweet taste and velvety skin, this most sensuous of fruits made its way west along the Silk Road and into the Middle East. Here the apricot may have gained a religious significance. Some biblical scholars think that the 'apple' plucked by Eve from the Tree of Knowledge of Good and Evil in the Garden in Eden and offered to Adam was in fact an apricot. Similarly, King Solomon was probably referring to apricots when he said 'comfort me with apples, for I am sick of love'.

It was from Persia that Alexander the Great is thought to have introduced the apricot to Greece in the 4th century BC, but it was from Armenia that a Roman general – either Lucullus or Pompey – brought trees to Italy so that the Romans were cultivating the fruit by the 1st century BC. Pliny, in the 1st century AD, refers to the 'Armenian plum'.

The apricot finally arrived in Britain in 1542, imported from Italy by John Wolf on the command of Henry VIII, who desired the fruit for the aphrodisiacal properties which it allegedly possessed. The apricot's shape may have been one reason why this virtue was ascribed to it, and why the medieval French word 'abricot' was apparently slang for vulva. The first English literary record of the 'Abricock', or the 'hasty peach', is found in William Turner's *The Names of Herbes* (1548), who adds that 'we have very fewe of these trees as yet'. Apricots remained relatively uncommon into the 17th century: in 1688 Leonard Meager of the Brompton Park Nursery in London offered seven cultivars for sale (even today the National Fruit Collection lists only 11). Perhaps the most famous – it appears in Jane Austen's *Mansfield Park* (1814) – was 'Moorpark', which was introduced from the continent by Admiral Lord Anson in 1760 and fruited for the first time in England at Moor Park in Hertfordshire. Both 'Moorpark and 'Early Moorpark', which ripens about a week earlier, are still available.

Indeed, Hertfordshire can lay claim to the title 'apricot county'. 'New Large Early', which dates from 1873, was raised in the Rivers Nursery of Sawbridgeworth by Thomas Rivers (1797–1877). The third generation of that name, he consolidated the fame of the family nursery established in 1725 (it closed for business as recently as 1985) and pursued a passion for breeding fruit trees. According to The Rivers Nursery Site & Orchard Group, Thomas was responsible for breeding 31 peach and 16 nectarine cultivars, over 20 new plums and six pears, as well as various apricots, cherries, raspberries and strawberries.

OPPOSITE *Apricot 'New Large Early' (with peach 'Peregrine' in bowl).*

CHERRY

Cultivated cherries are divided into sweet cherries, which derive from Prunus avium *(the wild cherry, mazzard or gean), a native to Britain, Europe and western Asia, and acid or sour cherries, which descend from* Prunus cerasus, *a tree native to much of Europe and southwest Asia that produces a fruit that is acid or tart. The vast majority of cultivated cherries are cultivars of the sweet cherry.*

SWEET CHERRY
Prunus avium

Fruit of the sweet cherry was gathered from the wild as early as the Mesolithic or Middle Stone Age period (*c.* 9660–5000 BC) in Denmark, and archaeological sites in England have yielded sweet cherry stones from the Bronze Age (*c.* 2500–800 BC). The increasing occurrence of remains in the Romano-British archaeological record is indicative of the growing popularity of the fruit. Mentioned neither in the *Læcboc of Bald* nor the *Lacnunga*, the first British literary reference is by Ælfric in the 10th century. By the Middle Ages, however, it seems the cherry was very popular and appears in numerous surviving records. At Ely in Cambridgeshire the Abbey grounds boasted a famous vineyard, and in 1302 there is mention of 'cherries in the vineyard sold'.

In 1573 Thomas Tusser's *Five hundred pointes of good husbandrie* lists simply red and black cherries. A little later Gerard describes 12 types, including the Flanders, Spanish, Gascoine, Late Ripe and Cluster, and he extols the many culinary virtues of the fruit. Cherries continued to be a favourite of both ordinary people and royalty – when Queen Elizabeth I made her Progress in 1599, Sir Frances Carew (see also p. 50) contrived to delay ripening by almost two months by using wetted fabric-covered frames so that he could serve cherries to Her Majesty upon her arrival in August.

In the early 17th century Parkinson lists 20 types, and complains of the difficulties of purchasing trees true to their name. That there was such confusion makes the task undertaken by John Gibson even more daunting. In 1768 this doctor and keen horticulturist set out to identify the various cherry cultivars grown in Italy and described by Pliny, publishing his results in *The Fruit-Gardener*. While he may not always be accurate, he concluded that Pliny's 'Duracina' is the French 'bigarot', of which a number of cultivars, including 'Bigarreau Antoine Nomblot'

and 'Bigarreau Gaucher', still survive. One new cherry cultivar of the 18th century is 'Black Tartarian', of Ukrainian origin. Still in commercial cultivation this produces a tender, dark-red fruit with full-bodied flavour and attractive purplish-black skin.

The doyen of early 19th-century cherry breeding was Thomas Andrew Knight (1759–1838) of Downton Castle in Herefordshire, a founder and later president of the (Royal) Horticultural Society. Using his large estate as his laboratory, he bred many successful new cultivars of various fruits, including cherry 'Elton Heart' (1806), 'Knight's Early Black' (*c.* 1810), 'Waterloo' (1815) and 'Knight's Bigarreau', all of which are still grown. To add to this wealth of new cherries, 'Bigarreau Napoléon' (syn. 'Napoléon') was introduced into Britain in 1832.

Another successful breeder was Thomas Ingram, head gardener to Queen Victoria at Frogmore, on the Windsor estate. In *c.* 1864 he released 'Frogmore Early', which has a red and yellow skin and pale yellow flesh that is very juicy and has a good flavour. An American import was 'Ronald's Heart', which produces a large, black, sweet-tasting fruit early in the season. By the end of the 19th century head gardeners were growing hundreds of different cultivars, and orchards covered the countryside. So famous were the cherry orchards along the banks of the River Tamar, on the Devon–Cornwall border, that in the early 20th century boat trips ran each spring to take tourists to admire the shows of blossom.

OPPOSITE, CLOCKWISE FROM ABOVE LEFT *Cherries 'Bigarreau Napoléon'; 'Knight's Bigarreau'; 'Black Tartarian' (in cask and right) and 'Ronald's Heart'; 'Frogmore Early'.*

CHERRY

ACID OR SOUR CHERRY
Prunus cerasus

The acid cherry is naturally a low-growing tree or shrub, from which cultivated acid cherries, like all fruit domesticated from the wild, would have been selected and subsequently bred to produce trees whose fruits had the desired character traits. It is likely the domestication of the acid cherry took place alongside that of the sweet cherry, somewhere in the vicinity of the Caspian and Black seas. In the late 8th century BC the Assyrian King Sargon II enjoyed either the scent of cherry blossom or the perfume-like aromas of the acid cherry fruits and the name cherry ultimately derives from the Akkadian, *karshu*, leading to the Greek *kerasus* and the Latin *cerasum*.

Known to the Greeks by 300 BC, the acid cherry was probably introduced to Britain by the Romans. However, the British palate has never appreciated the tartness of the acid cherry as much as the flavour of the sweet cherry, hence little effort was made to breed new cultivars. The fruit, as with so many others, did enjoy a fillip under Henry VIII, and by 1640 over two dozen named cultivars were grown; yet the number has always been low in comparison with sweet cherries.

Today, acid cherries are often divided into two groups. The clear-juice or Amarelle types have red pigment in the skin and translucent flesh. Heritage cultivars include 'Flemish Red' (syn. 'Flemish') and 'Kentish Red', which is very similar to the first but has larger fruits and ripens earlier in July. Both may have been brought back from Flanders by Richard Harris in 1533 (see p. 16). John Gibson in his attempt to identify the types of cherries discussed by Pliny (see sweet cherry) suggested that the 'Ceciliana' is the 'Kentish-cherry', which is perhaps the same as 'Kentish Red'. From France but dating to the 17th century is 'Montmorency'. The second group is the coloured-juice or Morello types, which have pigmented skin and flesh. The cultivar 'Morello', the most familiar of all acid cherries, is of Kentish origin and dates to the 16th century. The fruits of the acid or sour cherry are mostly used in cooking and also for liqueurs, the most famous of which is of course the German kirsch.

OPPOSITE *Cherry 'Morello'*.

CITRUS

The genus Citrus *has a genetic 'hot spot' in the region of southeast Asia bordered by the province of Yunnan in China, Burma and northeastern India, and it is widely held that this is where it originated. The word 'citrus' is of Greek derivation, from* kedros, *meaning cedar, one theory being that this refers to the use by Hellenistic Jews of the citron instead of the cedar cone during the biblical festival of Sukkot, or the Feast of the Tabernacles.*

CITRON
Citrus medica

The archaeological record reveals that the first citrus to be domesticated was the citron. In cultivation in China by around 4000 BC, from there it travelled west along trade routes. Known to the ancient Egyptians and the Sumerians by 2500 BC, it acquired the name Median or Persian apple. There is speculation that the word *hadar* spoken by Moses in Leviticus (23:40) is a derivation of the Assyrian *adaru*, meaning citron: 'You shall take, on the first day, fruits of the tree *hadar*, of palm branches, boughs of the thickest trees, and willows that cross the length of rapid waters and rejoice before the Lord your God'.

The citron was described in the late 4th century BC by Theophrastus and was known to the Romans. By the 10th century AD it was well established as a crop in Italy. From Salerno in 1003 for example, citron fruits (*poma cedrina*) were sent as a gift to the Norman lords who had saved the local ruler from the Saracens. The citron was mentioned by Albertus Magnus in the 13th century and by William Turner in the 16th century, who called the fruits 'Cytrones'. According to Parkinson it was widely grown by the 1620s.

The cultivar known as the 'Greek citron', which produces medium- to large-sized, bumpy yellow-skinned fruits with a very acidic flavour, was botanically classified by the German botanist Adolf Engler as the 'variety etrog'. Originally cultivated on the Ionian islands, predominantly Corfu, this cultivar became widely planted in Israel and gained its new name 'Etrog', the Hebrew word for citron. The citron is one of the four plants named in the Torah to be used as part of the celebration of Sukkot, the other three being a ripe closed frond from a date palm, leaved branches from the myrtle and leaved branches from the willow. The cultivar 'Etrog' is one of those accepted as a ritual etrog.

OPPOSITE *Citron 'Etrog'.*

CITRUS

ORANGE

Citrus aurantium & *Citrus sinensis*

Regarded as a natural hybrid that arose in southeastern Asia, the bitter orange reached China from India in about 2200 BC. The earliest literary reference to an orange (indeed any citrus fruit) so far known is contained in the chapter Yu Kung (or Tribute of Yu – the legendary ruler Da Yu) within the book *Shu Jing*, or Classic of History, dating to the 5th century BC, which reads: 'The baskets were filled with woven ornamental silks. The bundle contained small oranges and pummeloes.' The bitter orange made its way west with other citrus fruits and was familiar to the Romans, but in the aftermath of the collapse of the Roman empire, it was the Arab empire that was responsible for spreading this fruit far and wide. During the 10th century its cultivation reached Persia, Iraq, Syria, Palestine and Egypt, and subsequently northern Africa, Sicily, Sardinia and Spain. Further north, in England, the orange is named by Neckam in the late 13th century. Doubts have been raised about the possibility of the orange being grown in England at such an early date, but Neckam's lists are otherwise sound. Moreover the climate was then experiencing what is known as the Medieval Warm Period, which could have allowed orange cultivation, and it is perfectly possible that seeds of the bitter orange were brought to England by returning Crusaders. On the European mainland the bitter orange was first described in the late 13th century by Albertus Magnus, who noted that the tree was larger and more cold tolerant than the citron. Magnus's description is also the first to use the term *arangus* or orange.

The first substantiated record of bitter oranges reaching England dates from 1290 when Queen Eleanor of Castile (see p. 15) purchased seven from a Spanish ship that had berthed at Southampton carrying a cargo of the fruit. There is also an orange story associated with another Eleanor of Castile, the wife of Charles III of Navarre. This Eleanor grew an orange tree in a tub in Pamplona in Spain; in 1523 the tree became the property of Charles, Duke of Bourbon, and was subsequently confiscated by the Queen Mother, Louise of Savoy, who had it moved into her new orangerie at the palace of Fontainebleau in France. From there, a century or so later, it was transferred into the splendid, newly built orangerie at Versailles, where it eventually died in 1858, having never borne a fruit.

In medieval and early Tudor England citrus in general remained a novelty, available only to the wealthy as imported fruits. They also retained their royal association: the orange, lemon and citron are mentioned by John Lydgate in his poem 'Pur le Roy' that celebrates the entry of Henry VI into London in 1432:

> *Ther were eke treen, with leves fressh of hewe,*
> *Alle tyme of yeer, fulle of fruytes lade,*
> *Of colour hevynly, and ever-yliche newe,*
> *Orenges, almondis, and the pomegernade,*
> *Lymons, dates, theire colours fressh and glade,*
> *Pypyns, quynces, blaunderell [apple] to disport,*
> *And the pomecedre [citron] corageous to recomfort.*

By the reign of Elizabeth I, oranges had become more commonplace. Shakespeare refers to them several times, for instance in *Much Ado About Nothing* (see p. 50), first performed in 1598–99, and also in *Coriolanus*, which was probably first performed between late 1609 and early 1610: 'You know neither me, yourselves, nor anything. You are ambitious for

OPPOSITE *Orange 'Valencia'.*

The count is neither sad, nor sick, nor merry, nor well; but civil count, civil as an orange, and something of that jealous complexion.

Shakespeare, *Much Ado About Nothing*

poor knaves' caps and legs: you wear out a good wholesome forenoon in hearing a cause between an orange-wife and a fosset-seller.'

However, these oranges were not the bitter orange but the sweet orange (*Citrus sinensis*), whose origins are somewhat obscure. It appears to have arisen in southern China, possibly a hybrid between the pomelo (*C. maxima*) and mandarin (*C. reticulata*), and to have been in cultivation by 2500 BC. Its name in Sanskrit is *nagaranga*, meaning 'food that elephants like', revealing that it was known in India, but when and how it arrived in Europe is still a contentious topic. Some theorize that the Romans were aware of it; others have it brought west sometime after the 11th century by Genoese merchants who traded in Arabia, Palestine or India. A third school of thought believes the fruit travelled north from North Africa with the Arabs, and yet a fourth opinion maintains it was introduced by the Portuguese from India following Vasco de Gama's rounding of the Cape of Good Hope in 1497. The last theory seems least likely since there is evidence that the sweet orange was already well established in southern Europe by the early 16th century. Leandro Alberti, the Italian Dominican historian who travelled around Italy in 1523 wrote that he had observed vast groves of many different cultivars of orange trees (and lemon and citron) in Sicily, Calabria and Liguria – the majority of which had sweet fruit.

Imported fruit of the sweet orange was certainly familiar to the English by the end of the 16th century. In the 17th century, before she became a celebrated actor and later the mistress of King Charles II, Nell Gwyn had been an orange-girl selling her wares in the Theatre Royal in Drury Lane, London, indicating that the fruit was by then popular and the price not exorbitant.

As a cultivated garden plant the orange of either kind remained rare. The first person successfully to raise orange plants from seed in England was Sir Francis Carew of Beddington Park, whose bitter orange seedlings were thriving by 1580. John Gerard lists an 'arange, or Orange tree' among the plants in his garden in the 1590s, yet almost a century later the ever-inquisitive Samuel Pepys noted in his *Diary* for 19 April 1664 that he had walked 'with Creed and Vernaty in the Physique Garden in St. James's Parke; where I first saw orange-trees, and other fine trees'.

The orange and other citrus were grown as novel and expensive ornamentals rather than as fruit trees cultivated for a crop, and throughout the 18th century they remained a fad among those elite who could afford both the trees and the requisite growing conditions – specifically a heated shelter in the winter. But because of the orange's ornamental status, this heated shelter was not a glasshouse in the productive gardens, but a new form of ornate garden building positioned within the designed garden or landscape. Thus it was that the orange stimulated the fashion for the orangerie, an architectural structure often of Classical inspiration that was also home to tender ornamentals and provided a location for dining and entertaining. Over time, as the orangerie evolved into the exotic-filled conservatories and winter gardens of the 19th century, so the orange fell from fashion. Possibly because so many new and even more exciting and expensive tender exotic plants had arrived from the four corners of the world, the poor old orange simply became passé.

For those who wish to grow the tree for a crop of oranges the cultivar 'Valencia' is recommended. Named for that city in Spain, it in fact originates from California where it was bred in the first half of the 19th century by the pioneering agronomist William Wolfskill on his farm in Santa Ana. It is the groves of this cultivar that inspired the name Orange County. With an excellent, sweet flavour, it is widely cultivated around the world for juice production, and it is also useful because it is the only orange to flower in summer, and produces fruit at the same time.

OPPOSITE *Orange 'Valencia'*.

As my complaint has something in it that at least putts me in mind of the scurvy I took up the lemon Juice put up by Dr Hulmes direction … The small [cask] in which was lemon juice with one fifth of brandy was also very good … this therefore I began to make use of immediately drinking very weak punch made with it for my common liquor.

Banks, 1 April 1769

CITRUS

LEMON
Citrus limon

Members of the genus *Citrus* hybridize easily, and the lemon, like the orange, is also thought to have originated as a natural hybrid in southeastern Asia. The first Chinese literary evidence known is a surprisingly recent AD 1175, in the preface of the geographical treatise *Gui Hai Yu Heng Chi* written by Fan Chengda, a famous poet of the Song Dynasty. By this date the lemon had already been in cultivation for centuries and had arrived in regions further west. The Romans certainly knew the lemon and depicted it in their art. Murals from Pompeii, the town buried by the eruption of Vesuvius in AD 79, as well as a mosaic from 2nd-century Carthage in North Africa, show fruiting branches of lemon (and citron and orange). More evidence for citrus cultivation in Italy dates to the 4th century and an early Christian mausoleum built in Rome by the Constantine the Great for his half-sister Flavia Julia Constantia, who died in 330. A mosaic on the vaulted ceiling clearly shows citrons, lemons and oranges attached to freshly cut, leafy branches.

Neckam lists the lemon as grown in England by *c.* 1180 and Lydgate's poem quoted on p. 49 provides a mid-15th-century reference. However, there is a general scarcity of information relating to lemon cultivation in our usual sources, though Parkinson in 1629 notes that he has seen lemons 'in divers places'. With its sour fruit, the lemon was perhaps not as popular as the sweet orange, and its earliest uses may have been mostly medicinal. And even before 1825 and the invention of the gin and tonic, the lemon had already made an appearance as an addition to drinks, though also in a medicinal context. The botanist Sir Joseph Banks consumed a concoction of brandy and lemon juice in order to prevent scurvy during his travels aboard *Endeavour*, when he accompanied Lieutenant James Cook between 1768 and 1771, as recorded in his *Journal*.

As with oranges, lemons were taken to the Americas after the arrival of Columbus, and now form an important commercial crop in Florida and California in particular, though the industry suffered badly in the 'great freeze' of 1894–95. A popular heritage variety of lemon is 'Eureka', which originated in California in 1858, grown from seeds imported from Sicily. From an early age it produces an abundance of juicy fruit, with few pips, all year round.

OPPOSITE *Lemon 'Eureka'.*

CITRUS

LIME
Citrus aurantifolia & C. × latifolia

With its ripe yellow fruits, the lime, or Mexican or Key lime (*C. aurantifolia*), arrived in England in the 17th century and was growing in the Oxford Physic Garden by 1648, when it is included in a catalogue of about 1,600 plants being cultivated within the garden walls at that time. The catalogue was the work of the first Keeper, Jacob Bobart the Elder (*c.* 1599–1680), who, it is apocryphally claimed, kept a pet goat that would follow him around the garden. This lime, also probably a hybrid from south and southeastern Asia, was spread through India to Persia, Palestine and Egypt and then brought to Europe by the Arabs during the 13th century.

In the 19th century British sailors were given the nickname 'limeys' by Americans because of the Royal Navy's practice of issuing lime juice to sailors to prevent the potentially fatal disease scurvy, caused by vitamin deficiency. Limes replaced lemons as a source of Vitamin C-rich juice because the fruits were readily available from plantations established on British Caribbean colonies. The lime was also introduced to mainland America, flourishing in both Mexico and the Florida Keys, hence its popular names.

Incidentally, it is also from the West Indies that another citrus, the grapefruit (*C. × paradisi*), originates. This is a hybrid between the pomelo and sweet orange that occurred probably sometime in the 18th century, and was first referred to by the Reverend Griffith Hughes, author of *The Natural History of Barbados*, as the 'forbidden fruit' growing on that island in 1750.

The Tahiti lime (*C. × latifolia*), with its green fruits, is also known as the Persian lime. Presumed to be a hybrid of the lime and citron which may have originated in Thailand, this is a lime that has liked to travel. From Thailand it journeyed to the Mediterranean region via Persia. It is thought that from Greece it then went to Djerba, an island off the coast of Tunisia. For here grew an identical lime called 'Sakhesli', which translates as 'from Sakhos', an old Arabic name for the Greek island of Chios. It is thought that Portuguese traders took this lime to Brazil, from where it was transported to Australia in *c.* 1824 and then returned across the Atlantic to North America, specifically California, via Tahiti, between 1850 and 1880.

OPPOSITE *Tahiti lime.*

CURRANTS

All the cultivated currants are members of the genus Ribes, *which contains about 150 species including also the gooseberry and many ornamental plants. Currants require cool conditions in order to produce a crop and so were not known to Classical authors or grown by Mediterranean gardeners. However, the word 'currant' derives from Corinth because of the similar appearance of the fruit of* Ribes *to the small dried grape that took its name from that ancient Greek city.*

REDCURRANT & WHITECURRANT
Ribes rubrum

The redcurrant is native to central and northern mainland Europe and Asia, but not to Britain. The fact that it does not appear in any medieval texts as a cultivated plant, together with evidence from later literary sources, indicates that the redcurrant was domesticated in the 15th century. The first drawing of the plant appears in a *Herbarius* printed in Mainz in 1484. More references are found in the 16th century, including by Johannes Ruellius in *De natura stirpium libri tres* (1536) and Matthiolus in the 1548 edition of his *Commentarii*, as well as an illustration in *De Historia Stirpium* (1542) by the German physician Leonhart Fuchs (1501–66). These authors indicate that the redcurrant was particularly popular in Holland.

The first English account is by Turner, in *The Names of Herbes* in 1548, who says that in some parts of England it is called a 'Rasin tree'. Gerard was growing both redcurrants and whitecurrants in his garden in the 1590s (and black – see p. 58). The great plant collector John Tradescant the Elder introduced a 'Great Red currant' from Holland in 1611, and the large-berried cultivars that were developed in the 17th century in both Belgium and northern France also found their way across the channel.

Over the course of the next four centuries new currant cultivars were developed, but not in as great numbers as for example the gooseberry (see p. 61). In 1810 Thomas Andrew Knight began to work on redcurrants and whitecurrants but did not achieve the same success as he did with cherries (see p. 45), and those cultivars he did breed have sadly disappeared. The redcurrant 'Wilson's Long Bunch' (syn. 'Victoria') is a 19th-century English introduction and produces a good harvest of small berries late in the season.

The whitecurrant (also known as the pink or yellow currant) is considered an albino variant of the redcurrant and shares the same history. The cultivar 'Versailles' was raised in about 1835 by the Frenchman M. Bertin who resided in the town of the same name as his currant. It produces a large, sweet, yellowish fruit in early July. Pinkcurrants such as 'Rosa Hollandische' are hybrids between red and white cultivars.

OPPOSITE: ABOVE *Whitecurrant 'Versailles'*; BELOW LEFT *redcurrant 'Wilson's Long Bunch'*; BELOW RIGHT *pinkcurrant 'Rosa Hollandische'*.

The black Curran bush riseth higher than the white … the flowers
are also like unto little bottles as the others be … both branches,
leaves, and fruit have a kind of stinking sent with them …
but the berries are eaten of many, without offending
either taste or smell.

Parkinson, 1629

CURRANTS

BLACKCURRANT

Ribes nigrum

This small shrub with its fragrant (or pungent, depending on your taste) leaves and stems is, as with the redcurrant, native to northern Europe and northern Asia but not Britain. In fact, also like the redcurrant, it is quite a late arrival to the English garden. Some authorities claim that the blackcurrant was first cultivated at Hatfield House by Sir Robert Cecil, the bushes having been brought from the continent by John Tradescant the Elder. It is true that a bill of purchase for 'on dussin of great blacke currants' dated 5 January 1611 and for the sum of 1s has survived, but there is an earlier record of the blackcurrant in cultivation. Gerard (1599) includes '*Ribes nigra*' (along with *R. alba* and *R. rubra*) in the list of plants that he was growing in his Holborn garden.

In the 17th century John Parkinson (1629) was an admirer of the blackcurrant (see quote), but he was a lone voice. The fruit's distinct flavour proved unpopular, with author after author stating that it was not worth planting. It was not until the late 18th century, and on medicinal grounds, that the blackcurrant was rehabilitated. Its popularity increased through the 19th century and one of the favourite new cultivars was 'Black Naples', which was in cultivation by 1826 and remains so. Another favourite that remains available is 'Lee's Prolific', which was introduced in 1860 by the market gardener George Lee of Clevedon in Somerset. The cultivar 'Blacksmith' was introduced by the nurserymen Messrs Laxton Brothers of Bedford in 1916 and is highly productive.

The British love of blackcurrant cordial dates to the Second World War and a government policy. In the absence of fruits containing high levels of Vitamin C, blackcurrant cultivation was encouraged across the country and from 1942 almost the entire crop was processed into syrup and distributed free to children. Even today the great majority of the British harvest goes into the manufacture of Ribena. The French, on the other hand, turn blackcurrants into the sweet, strong-tasting liqueur crème de cassis, especially used to flavour kir.

OPPOSITE *Blackcurrant 'Blacksmith'*.

GOOSEBERRY

Ribes uva-crispa

The gooseberry, a straggling bush with long, sharp spines along the stems, is native to northwest Africa, southwestern Asia and Europe, including Britain. As with the other cultivated members of the genus *Ribes* the gooseberry is a cool weather fruit and was thus unknown to the Classical authors, who lived and wrote in warmer, southern climes. Where it grew naturally, wild fruit was no doubt harvested from ancient times, but perhaps surprisingly the gooseberry does not appear in any of the early English literary sources, though it is mentioned on the continent by Albertus Magnus in the later 13th century. The first record of a cultivated gooseberry is a 1275 royal account of *greseiller* bushes purchased at a cost of 3d each for Edward I's ornamental garden or herber at Tower Hill.

In 1509, the first year of Henry VIII's reign, a 'pale' cultivar was introduced from Flanders, and in 1548 Turner discusses the gooseberry, saying it was a garden plant in England but cultivated in the fields in Germany among other bushes. Gerard (1597) states that the gooseberry is widely cultivated in gardens and makes note of 'divers sorts', saying 'wee have three red Gooseberries, a blew and a greene', adding that it is also called Feaberrie bush. Parkinson (1629) also uses both the traditional English name Feaberrie as well as the one we know today. It is thought that 'gooseberry' may be a derivation from *kruisbezie*, the Dutch word for the fruit. As with currants, the gooseberry was much improved by Dutch growers in the 17th century. The first to name individual gooseberries was John Rea in his *Flora* (1665), and of these 'Hedgehog' continues to be cultivated. Also of 17th-century origin is the red-berried 'Ironmonger'.

In the second half of the 18th century the gooseberry acquired cult status among Lancastrian industrial workers, who established Gooseberry Clubs, bred literally hundreds of new cultivars and exhibited the fruits of their labours at special gooseberry shows. These competitions were taken very seriously, and from 1786 an annual *Gooseberry Grower's Register* was published, recording the names of the prizewinners, the varieties grown and the weights of the berries – which was the criterion on which the competitions were judged. In later years the records of berry weights provided Charles Darwin with data that he made use of in *The Variation of Plants and Animals under Domestication* (1868).

As a result of the enthusiasm of Gooseberry Club members, the numbers of available cultivars rose dramatically. In 1826 the (Royal) Horticultural Society garden at Chiswick grew 185 cultivars, a number that had risen to 360 by 1831. And in that same year George Lindley, in *A Guide to the Orchard and Fruit Garden* (edited by John Lindley), observed that 'the gentlemen of Lancashire … have given premiums for several years, for raising curious new sorts, remarkable for size and flavour'. He also listed 'two hundred of the principal' cultivars exhibited between 1825 and 1829, divided by fruit colour into reds, yellows, greens and whites. This is followed by a second list, naming a further 722 'Additional Gooseberries cultivated in this Country'. Very few of these nearly 1,000 named cultivars remain in cultivation; one that does, however, is 'Whitesmith' (syn. 'Woodward's Whitesmith'), raised by Mr Woodward before 1824.

The fashion for gooseberry breeding declined dramatically in the second half of the 19th century, but new cultivars continued to be introduced. For instance 'Leveller' (1851) is a green-fruited cultivar raised by J. Greenhalgh of Ashton-under-Lyne in Staffordshire. Producing paler green fruits is 'Careless', raised by Mr Crompton and in cultivation by 1860. Acquired by the National Fruit Collection in the 1950s 'Black Seedling' and 'Lord Derby' are both red-berried cultivars, the latter being one of the latest to ripen.

OPPOSITE *Gooseberries 'Whitesmith', 'Ironmonger' and 'Careless' (top to bottom).*

ABOVE *Gooseberry 'Leveller'.*

ABOVE *Gooseberry 'Lord Derby'.*

HOTHOUSE FRUIT

Archaeological evidence reveals that the peach and fig were introduced into England by the Romans, and archival sources show that they were in cultivation in early medieval gardens. The nectarine was a late-comer, arriving in the 17th century. At this time these fruits were cultivated outdoors as wall and orchard fruit. However, from the 18th century onwards they also found a warm welcome within the confines of hothouses, and as cultural regimes improved so the peach, nectarine and fig were 'forced' to produce a harvest outside their natural season.

PEACH & NECTARINE
Prunus persica & *P. persica* var. *nectarina*

The Greek authors Theophrastus and, later, Dioscorides, as well as the Roman writers Columella and Pliny all believed the peach to be of Persian origin, as the species name suggests. But despite the insistence of such authorities, the peach is in fact indigenous to northern China. It plays an important role in Chinese mythology, the fruit being the symbol of longevity, and peach blossom features in Chinese poetry. Literary accounts of peach cultivation in China begin with *Shi Jing* (Book of Songs) written around 1000 BC. The Chinese archaeological record reveals peach stones from a site in Wu County in Jiansu Province that date back to the 5th millennium BC.

From its homeland the peach travelled west along the Silk Road into India and western Asia. It was reputedly brought to Europe by Alexander the Great and his troops, who encountered the fruit in Persia (hence the confusion among Classical writers concerning its origin). China remains home to many wild hybrid forms of downy-skinned peach, with different coloured skins and flesh. However, the smooth-skinned variety, known as the nectarine, is indigenous to east Turkestan.

It was the Romans who introduced the peach to Britain and it appears in most of the early and medieval texts, beginning in the 10th century with both the *Læcboc of Bald* and the *Lacnunga*, in which it is called *persoces*. Alexander Neckam in the late 13th century also refers to the peach, but it appears to have been a relatively uncommon fruit, restricted to the gardens of the wealthy – in monasteries and the houses of the nobility and royalty – where it enjoyed great popularity. However, this partiality was not always to the good – as already noted (p. 16), it is said that King John died after eating a surfeit of unripe peaches in 1216. Undaunted, his

OPPOSITE *Peaches 'Rochester' and 'Peregrine' (in bowl).*

> I presume the name Nucipersica doth most rightly belong unto that kinde of Peach which we call Nectorins, and although they have beene with us not many yeares, yet have they beene knowne in Italy to Matthiolus and others before him.

> Parkinson, 1629

grandson Edward I planted two peach trees in the gardens at Tower Hill in London in 1275 at the cost of a shilling each.

It is likely that the cultivation of the peach, along with that of other tree fruits, declined in the 14th and 15th centuries as a result of the combination of the impact of the Black Death and the cooler climate that followed the end of the Medieval Warm Period (a chilling that also marked the end of vine cultivation in northerly latitudes). New cultivars were subsequently introduced during the reign of Henry VIII. Even so, Thomas Tusser (1580 edition) names only red and white types, and Gerard (1597) was able to describe just four – white, red, 'd'auunt' (avant) and yellow – referring to skin and flesh colour.

In the next few decades the popularity of the peach increased and the nectarine arrived – the first mention of the latter in an English text dates to 1616 according to the *Oxford English Dictionary*, in which the fruits were called 'nectaryas'. By 1629 John Parkinson records 21 peach cultivars, including the 'Carnation Peach', the 'Newington Peach', the 'Melocotone Peach' and the 'Nutmeg Peach', adding: 'Many other sorts of Peaches there are, whereunto wee can give no especiall name; and therefore I passe them over in silence'. He also can list six nectarine cultivars. Parkinson was sufficiently familiar with the word 'peach' to use it as an adjective to describe the flower colour of ornamentals. Numbers of cultivars increased, and John Rea in 1676 lists 35 types of peach and 11 nectarines. Although when Mawe compiled his list (9th ed., 1782) he could only give 23 kinds of peaches, by 1831 a total of 183 varieties were grown by the (Royal) Horticultural Society in its Chiswick garden.

As with so many other fruits, the man who had the greatest impact on peach and nectarine breeding in the 19th century was Thomas Rivers (see p. 41). Three of his finest nectarine introductions that remain available today are 'Lord Napier' (1860), with dark crimson-flushed skin and white flesh, which was raised from an 'Early Albert' peach seedling, 'Sea Eagle' (1881) and 'Early Rivers' (1893). The Rivers' legacy lived on after his death, and in the early years of the 20th century the nursery introduced peach 'Duke of York' and peach 'Peregrine' in 1906. The latter, raised from a 'Spenser' nectarine seedling, is still a firm favourite, with white flesh and an excellent flavour. The peach was taken to America by the Spanish and became an important commercial crop from the 19th century. Yellow-fruited 'Rochester' is a very popular American cultivar dating from 1900. Both 'Peregrine' and 'Rochester' are recommended for glasshouse growing, but may also be cultivated outdoors in favourable areas, the former as a wall fruit and the latter as a bush fruit.

OPPOSITE *Nectarine 'Lord Napier'.*

HOTHOUSE FRUIT

FIG
Ficus carica

The fig is cultivated for what is generally referred to as its fruit, but which botanically speaking is a 'syconium infructescence' or a false fruit formed of a specially adapted inflorescence, in this case an enlarged, fleshy, hollow receptacle within which multiple flowers and seeds grow together to form a single mass. The common fig is indigenous to an area that extends from the Mediterranean region west to India, and is one of the first fruits to have been cultivated by man. Carbonized fruits found in the Neolithic village of Gilgal I in the Jordan Valley date to between 11,200 and 11,400 years ago, and may be the first evidence of agriculture, predating the domestication of wheat by about a millennium. The fruit was cultivated and esteemed in ancient Egypt, where it was also often used as offerings in tombs and to the gods (the Sycomore fig, *F. sycamorus,* was sacred to Hathor). From Egypt the fig probably spread north via Crete to mainland Greece. The first authenticated European reference is by Archilochus, who tells of trees cultivated on the island of Paros by the 7th century BC.

In Jewish tradition, the fig is eaten during Passover celebrations. It is the third tree to be named in Genesis, after the Tree of Life and the Tree of Knowledge of Good and Evil, and its leaves were used by Adam and Eve to cover their nakedness after eating the fruit of the second named tree. In Greek 'sycophant' means fig-revealer or a person who shows the fig, and was originally used to mean a false-accuser or slanderer; it seems to have arisen when certain Athenians informed on others who were illegally exporting figs. One Greek myth describes how the 'fruit of autumn' – dried figs were an important part of the winter diet – was given to man by the goddess Demeter. But the fig was also sacred to bibulous and libidinous Dionysos, who carved (and used) a fig wood phallus as part of his agreement with Prosymnos for his assistance in retrieving his mother, Semele, from Hades. The Romans were great consumers of the fruit and a fig tree appears in the earliest Roman myth of Romulus and Remus. According to Pliny (who also described 29 types of figs), the sacred fig tree growing in the Forum in Rome was 'known as Ruminalis because the she-wolf was discovered beneath it giving her teats [*rumis*] to the infant boys'.

It was the Romans who brought the fig to Britain, and perhaps because of its religious symbolism two stories concerning the early planting of figs in England have ecclesiastical associations. Legend has it that in the middle of the 12th century Thomas Becket planted a fig at the Old Palace of the Archbishop of Canterbury at West Tarring in Sussex on his return from a pilgrimage to Rome; and another claim for the first fig tree grown in England is that planted by Cardinal Pole in the Archbishop's garden at Lambeth Palace in 1525. It was still growing in 1825 when John Claudius Loudon reported that it was a 'White Marseilles' fig – a cultivar which remains available today. A year after this the (Royal) Horticultural Society had 75 cultivars growing in its gardens at Chiswick.

Sadly, only a few heritage varieties have survived, of which the most famous is 'Brown Turkey' (syn. 'Large Blue'). In cultivation by 1777 and grown for its large brown pear-shaped fruit with rich sweet red flesh, this was the most widely grown fig, and although perfectly at home under glass it is also ideal for outdoor cultivation. Introduced by Messrs Osborn of the Fulham Nursery in 1879, 'Osborn's Prolific' produces a tasty large fruit with very attractive purplish-brown skin, and may in fact be a reintroduction of an older cultivar. Another old cultivar with dark red skin and wine red flesh is 'Violette de Bordeaux' (syn. 'Negronne'); it was certainly in cultivation before 1901. The 'St Ervan' figs are old cultivars whose names were lost and so far the RHS has not yet been able to identify them precisely.

OPPOSITE *Fig 'Brown Turkey'.*

In the flesh of the mulberry there is a juice of a vinous flavour, and the fruit assumes
three different colours, being at first white, then red, and ripe when black....
It is in this tree that human ingenuity has effected the least improvement of all;
there are no varieties here, no modifications effected by grafting, nor, in fact,
any other improvement except that the size of the fruit,
by careful management, has been increased.

Pliny, 1st century AD

MULBERRY
Morus nigra

The black mulberry is native to the southern Caucasus or Nepal, but has been cultivated for so long that its exact origins are lost in the mists of time. It was grown in Mesopotamia and ancient Egypt, and the tree is mentioned in four verses of the Old Testament (2 Samuel 5:23 and 24 and Chronicles 14:14 and 15). The mulberry was known to Theophrastus, and Pliny describes both the black and white species, and also gives the first Western description of silk production.

This is another fruit introduced to Britain by the Romans, and given that the tree will live upwards of 600 years it is unlikely that it fell from cultivation. It is listed in the *Læcboc of Bald* as *byrigberge*, and appears in numerous medieval accounts. For example, in the 12th century Gerard of Wales recounts how mulberry juice was served at a meal he had with the monks of Canterbury Cathedral Priory. In the same century and city, it was beneath a mulberry tree that the murderers of Thomas Becket left their cloaks and put on their swords in 1170. In 1241 a clerk to Henry III paid 6s 8d for mulberry and raspberry drinks for the king; and if the legend stating that the mulberry at Ribston in Yorkshire was brought back from the Crusades and planted by the Knights Templar is to be believed, this must have happened prior to the Templar suppression in 1312.

Although the mulberry has always been a popular tree it has never been widely planted only for its fruit; rather, the harvest is a bonus pro-duced by a particularly beautiful ornamental tree. There is one exception, and that was King James I's attempt to create an English silk industry (see p. 19). Unfortunately, black rather than white mulberries were planted and so it was an expensive mistake. James's own orchard of 4 acres (1.62 ha) established in 1608 on the site now occupied by Buckingham Palace cost him the huge sum of £1,935.

The mulberry is one fruit where nature does not require the improving hand of man, and few attempts have been made to develop new cultivars. In 1826 the (Royal) Horticultural Society garden in Chiswick boasted only five kinds, and the general opinion was that the only one worth growing was the species.

Two other species of mulberry are grown in Great Britain. The white mulberry (*M. alba*), native to the mountainous regions of central and eastern China, was growing in John Gerard's garden by 1599 and is best known as the preferred food of silkworms. The red mulberry (*M. rubra*), native to eastern North America, was discovered and introduced to Britain by John Tradescant the Younger (1608–62), and is a beautiful ornamental tree.

OPPOSITE *Black mulberry.*

> The Raspberry … produces agreeable eatable fruit …
> in estimation both as a dessert fruit to eat raw, and for making
> tarts, sauces, raspberry jam, and other culinary preparations,
> and therefore highly demands culture in every garden.
>
> Mawe, 1779

RASPBERRY

Rubus idaeus

The raspberry is a member of the diverse genus *Rubus*, and the word 'raspberry' originally meant (and for many still does) specifically the red-fruited species *R. idaeus*, which is native to northern Asia and Europe, including Britain. The species name derives from Mount Ida, southeast of ancient Troy in Turkey, where legend has it the ancient Greeks became familiar with the fruit. Botanically speaking, however, a raspberry is the fruit of any member of the *Rubus* subgenus *Idaeobatus*, which enjoys a global distribution. And the fruit is technically not a berry at all, but an aggregate fruit of numerous drupelets (fruits in which an outer fleshy part surrounds a hardened shell within which is the seed) around a central core.

Known to both the Greeks and the Romans, the raspberry was valued more as a medicine than an edible. Archaeological evidence reveals the consumption of raspberries in Britain dating back to the Bronze Age, the fruits gathered either from nature or from wild plants deliberately cultivated. However, the raspberry is absent from medieval literary sources, although the juice was a favourite of Henry III. Turner in 1548 states that 'raspeses', 'raspis' or 'hindberrie' was under cultivation in 'certayne gardines of Englande', and by 1629 Parkinson reports both red and white types. Later in the century the noted agriculturist John Worlidge (1640–1700) was a keen supporter of the raspberry, stating that the fruit should not be omitted from any garden. Nonetheless, until the last quarter of the 18th century the wild red and white forms remained the most widely cultivated types, with the sole named type being 'Large Red'.

By the turn of the 19th century, however, 'Yellow Antwerp' was in cultivation and indeed remains so. This was the creation of one of two nurserymen, either Mr North of Lambeth or Mr Maddock of Walworth.

By 1826 the (Royal) Horticultural Society's collection stood at a scanty 23 cultivars. In 1834 one of its recommended cultivars for planting in London was 'Red Antwerp', and it was this cultivar which in 1880 or 1881 was inadvertently hybridized with the American blackberry 'Aughinburgh' by lawyer and horticulturist James Harvey Logan of Santa Cruz, California, resulting in the loganberry.

Many old raspberry cultivars have been lost from cultivation. However, breeding work was undertaken at East Malling Research Station in Kent from the 1920s with the aim of developing new cultivars which possessed qualities of high yield and disease resistance. The first pioneering breeder was Norman H. Grubb, who was responsible for 'Malling Jewel' (among many other cultivars). Following his 30-year tenure he was succeeded by Drs Knight and Keep, who also developed numerous cultivars, among them 'Leo' (syn. 'Malling Leo').

All the raspberries so far mentioned are summer bearing, but there are also cultivars that crop in late summer or early autumn. The first mention of a late-fruiting raspberry is the 'twice-' or 'double-bearing' in the late 18th century. In *The British Fruit-Gardener* (1779), Mawe lists as 'Twice-Bearing' both a red and white raspberry, the latter improved by the French in the early 19th century. Also French and raised prior to 1850, the cultivar 'Belle de Fontenay' became one of the 19th century's most important autumn-raspberries. From the famous Veitch Nursery 'November Abundance' made its debut in the early 20th century and, more recently, East Malling experimented by using other raspberry species rather than cultivars as parents, resulting in the popular 'Autumn Bliss' (1984).

OPPOSITE *Raspberries 'Malling Jewel' (in punnet) and 'Leo'.*

Wife, into thy garden and set me a plot,
With strawberry roots the best to be got:
Such sowing abroad, among thorns in the wood,
Well chosen and picked, prove excellent good.

Tusser, 1577

STRAWBERRY

Fragaria × ananassa

The genus *Fragaria* contains about 20 species with a worldwide distribution. The wood strawberry (*F. vesca*) is native throughout the northern hemisphere including Britain, and archaeologists have discovered seeds in Mesolithic, Neolithic and Iron Age sites, suggesting consumption since earliest times. The common name may derive from one of a number of sources, favourites being the Anglo-Saxon *streoberie*, alternatively 'strewberries', referring to either their growth habit or the straw placed under them to protect the fruit, or 'straws of berries', from the way the fruits were sold like a kebab on a piece of straw. As with the raspberry, what we eat is in fact not a berry, though in this case it is a swollen receptacle (the platform for the flowering parts), on the outside of which are attached the achenes; inside each achene is a single seed.

Various Roman writers including Ovid, Pliny and Apicius mention *fraga* – but not as a cultivated crop. The strawberry is *streawberian* in the *Læcboc of Bald* and the *streawbergean* in *Lacnunga*. Perhaps because of its ubiquity, the strawberry was passed over by early ecclesiastical medieval authors, although it may also have been because the fruit was considered unwholesome by some. In the 12th century St Hildegard of Bingen declared strawberries unfit to eat because they grew on the ground where snakes and toads trod. Conversely, the strawberry has also been associated with love – its heart shape and red colour made it the symbol of Venus, and it has been used to symbolize purity, prosperity, peace, perfection and righteousness. The fruit is also believed by some to have healing qualities. One devotee was Madame Thérésa Tallien, a leading Parisian socialite and favourite at the court of Napoleon, who regularly bathed in the juice extracted from 10 kg (22 lb) of the fruit, though what was supposed to have been healed is not recounted.

The wood strawberry was planted extensively as an ornamental on the Mount in Henry VIII's Privy Garden at Hampton Court palace in the 1530s, and there is a story that the palace's previous owner, Cardinal Wolsey, was the first to serve strawberries and cream to his guests in 1509. Thomas Tusser's poem quoted above indicates the continuing practice of cultivating wood strawberry plants gathered from the wild, something that would not change for a further two centuries.

It is the French whom we must thank for the cultivated strawberry. The breakthrough that led to the modern, large-fruited strawberry came by accident in the mid-18th century, when a female *F. chiloensis* (large-fruiting Chilean type), which had been brought to Plougastel in Brittany from Concepción in Chile by the French spy Amédée-François Frézier, naturally hybridized with a male *F. virginiana* (from Virginia, North America). The result is now named *Fragaria × ananassa*, and is the ancestor of commercially grown types.

In 1884 Robert Hogg, the great cataloguer of fruits, lists 128 cultivars, including at least four developed by Thomas Ingram, the head gardener to Queen Victoria at Frogmore. But the 19th century's most successful British breeder of new varieties was Michael Keens, a market gardener of Isleworth, on the edge of London. His cultivars included 'Keens' Imperial' and 'Keens' Seedling', though sadly neither of these – nor most of those listed by Hogg – remain in cultivation. One excellent heritage variety that is still available is 'Royal Sovereign' (1892), which was bred by that most prolific of nurserymen, Thomas Laxton. Not only does this remain on the market, but it is still considered by many to be our best-flavoured cultivar.

OPPOSITE *Strawberry 'Royal Sovereign'.*

ALLIUMS

The genus Allium *contains about 750 species, with the centre of its diversity being Central Asia, from the Himalaya to Turkestan. The most important edible species are onion, shallots, garlic and leek (p. 210).*

ONION
Allium cepa

The English word 'onion' is thought to derive from the Latin *unio* or 'oneness', through the French 'oignon'. Onions were held in high esteem in ancient Egypt: Herodotus tells us in his *The Histories* (*c.* 430 BC) that 'engraved on the pyramid [of Cheops] is the amount spent on the workers in radishes, onions and garlic … this expense came to one thousand six hundred talents of silver'. John Evelyn in *Acetaria* (1699) reckoned this amount at 'Ninety Tun of Gold'. Small onions were placed in the eye sockets of pharaoh Ramesses IV during mummification, and garlic bulbs were found in the tomb of Tutankhamun. In addition, Pliny recounts that both onion and garlic were invoked as deities by Egyptians taking oaths. In the Bible (Numbers 11:5) the Israelites lament the meagre diet enforced by the Exodus: 'We remember the fish, which we did eat in Egypt freely, the cucumbers and the melons and the leeks and the onions and the garlic'. And it was not just the Egyptians and Israelites – numerous tablets of the Third Dynasty of Ur in Mesopotamia record the cultivation and distribution of onions. Even today the onion has enthusiastic followers: in Paris there is a formally registered religious sect known as the Worshippers of the Onion (congregation *c.* 4,000 at the end of the 20th century).

Although there is no firm archaeological evidence that the Romans introduced the onion and garlic to Britain, given that both were central to the Roman diet and grow readily in the islands it is a justifiable assumption that they did. The onion (as well as garlic and leek) is listed as *cipan* and *cipean* in the *Læcboc of Bald* and Ælfric's *Glossary*, indicating that if the Romans did not bring it, the onion was an early monastic introduction – and it has been a staple ever since. Gerard (1597) describes four types of onion: the white, red and Spanish, the last of which has a longer root, and the scallion. The scallion which 'hath but small roots, growing many together' is a description of the Welsh onion (*A. fistulosum*).

According to Evelyn 'an honest laborious Country-man, with good Bread, Salt, and a little Parsley, will make a contented Meal with a roasted Onion', and that the best 'are such as are brought us out of Spain, whence they of St. Omers had them'. St Omer is in northern France, and Alexandre Dumas proudly claims in his *Grand Dictionnaire de Cuisine* (1873) that Brittany was famous for growing onions, which were exported to England; even as recently as the 1970s I can remember as a child in Bristol my mother purchasing strings of onion from a bicycle-wheeling, beret-wearing Breton.

Of the heritage varieties still in cultivation, the white onion 'Bedfordshire Champion' was introduced by Suttons in 1869 and is 'One of the best & most popular of the large onions… One of the most reliable & a good keeper'. The decorative 'Red Brunswick' (syn. 'Dark Red Brunswick' and 'Brunswick Deep Blood-red') is listed as 'Rouge très Foncé de Brunswick' in Vilmorin's *Description des Plantes Potagères* (1856), where it is said to be remarkable for its colour; it also keeps well. Other heritage varieties include 'Paris Silver Skin' (syn. 'Blanc Hatif', by 1771), 'White Lisbon' (by 1787) and the perennially popular 'Ailsa Craig' (1887).

OPPOSITE *A pattern of onions and shallots.* OVERLEAF *Onions 'Red Brunswick' (bottom left) and 'Bedfordshire Champion' (centre) and shallot 'Cuisse de Poulet de Poitou' (top right).*

The breath of those that feed on [shallots] is not offensive to others, as it is of those who feed on Garlick or Onions.

Worlidge, 1683

ALLIUMS

SHALLOT

Allium cepa var. *aggregatum*

The shallot, or eschcalot, has nothing to do with Tennyson's poem about the Lady of Shalott. Rather, the French historian and journalist Joseph François Michaud (1767–1839) asserts that it was brought back from the Holy Land by the Crusaders. Indeed an older name and species synonym is *ascalonicum*, after Ashkelon, the port city in Palestine where Delilah cut the locks from Samson's head. Pliny mentions an Ascalonian onion, 'so called from Ascalon, a city of Judaea', but since he says it is best propagated from seed, whereas shallots are more usually grown from sets or divisions (though they can be grown from seed), he is perhaps referring to something else.

Michaud is backed up by the fact that the shallot does not appear on an English plant list until the Mayer manuscript of *c.* 1450. However, there is evidence from *Capitulare de Villis* that the shallot was being grown on the continent by the early 9th century, as 'ascalonicas' are listed alongside onions, leeks and garlic.

One of the distinguishing features of the shallot when compared with the onion is that is multiplies into numerous bulbs from the single one planted (like garlic also), and there is frequently a confusion with scallions, or the Welsh or bunching onion, in various sources. But it is perhaps the shallot that John Worlidge describes in his *Systema Horticulturae* (1683), when he writes 'Eschalots are now from France become an English condiment, and are increased and managed near after the same manner as the Garlick'. Batty Langley (1696–1751) also makes the association with garlic in his *New Principles of Gardening* (1728), saying 'Eschalots, or Shallots, being of the same Family with the Garlicks', adding 'They are of great Use in Sauces, and therefore a Kitchen Garden ought not to be without them'.

It seems the French have always favoured shallots more than the English, and one heritage cultivar is 'Cuisse de Poulet du Poitou' (syn. 'Zebrune'), which has a mild flavour and firm pink flesh. 'Cuisse de Poulet' means chicken thigh and refers to the elongated shape of this form of shallot, also known as banana shallots. There are also smaller, rounder shallots and the grey shallot, or 'échalote grise'.

OPPOSITE *Onion 'Red Brunswick' (left), shallot 'Cuisse de Poulet de Poitou' (centre) and onion 'Bedfordshire Champion' (right).*

Garlyke is not onlye good meat but also good medicine.

Turner, 1551

ALLIUMS

GARLIC

Allium sativum

The British native Ramsons, Crow Garlic or wild garlic (*A. ursinum*) has long been used in cookery, but the bulbous garlic is probably a Roman introduction. The name garlic derives from the Old English *garleac*, meaning 'spear leek'. It could also be argued that garlic, or the 'stinking rose' as it is often known, is more accurately classified as a herb than a vegetable, for many early writers from antiquity onwards cite more medicinal than culinary uses, and it was long thought to have antivenomous and other healing properties. Pliny listed many therapeutic attributes and Gerard in 1597 gives one name for garlic as 'husbandmans Treacle' – the original meaning of treacle was a medicinal compound.

Like other alliums, garlic's homeland was probably Central Asia, from where it spread widely. In addition to being in cultivation for thousands of years, garlic has an extensive mythology and folklore associated with it. It was sacred to the ancient Egyptians and in ancient Greece garlic was placed at cross-roads to supplicate the dark forces of the goddess Hecate. On Hermes' advice Odysseus munched it to avoid being turned into a pig by the sorceress Circe. Other religions and cultures, however, have eschewed garlic. An Islamic legend tells that when Satan stepped out from the Garden in Eden after the fall of man, garlic sprang up from the spot where he placed his left foot, and onion from where his right foot touched the ground.

Because of its perceived warming and stimulating effects garlic is shunned by Buddhists. For the same reason it is designated a 'yang' food by the Chinese, and was fed to Roman soldiers for added courage. This stimulatory effect was also alluded to by Aristotle, while the ancient Hebrew text, the *Talmud*, promotes garlic as an aphrodisiac. Folklore of course holds that garlic is *the* vampire repellant, and will protect against the Evil Eye; it also reputedly keeps away those jealous nymphs that terrorize pregnant women and engaged maidens.

Garlic is now an essential part of British cuisine and comes in two main types, softneck and hardneck (or rocambole). The cultivar 'Cristo' is a white-skinned French cultivar renowned for its particularly strong flavour. Bred on the Isle of Wight and the first garlic to ripen 'Early Wight' is best consumed soon after harvest.

OPPOSITE *Garlic 'Cristo'.*

BEANS

Beans are both an Old World and a New World crop, and one of the longest cultivated of all vegetables. Broad beans have been an important source of protein in the British diet since the Iron Age; in the medieval period they were primarily a field crop but were also grown in gardens and were consumed in a variety of ways, including bread made from bean flour.

BROAD, ENGLISH OR FAVA BEAN

Vicia faba

The broad bean, technically a vetch and native to North Africa and southwest Asia, was cultivated in the Aegean, Iberia and transalpine Europe by the 2nd millennium BC. Even Homer makes a passing mention of beans in Book XIII of *The Iliad*, and it appears in the myths and rituals of a number of different cultures. In Greek mythology Kyamites was a demi-god or hero of the Eleusinian Mysteries who presided over the cultivation of beans. Pliny stated that in the 'ancient ceremonials' of Rome 'bean pottage occupies its place in the religious services of the gods', but adds that the bean was condemned by Pythagorus in 'the belief which he entertained that the souls of the dead are enclosed in the bean', for which reason it was also used in funerals. In medieval England spitting a mouthful of beans into a witch's face was said to neutralize her powers. The bean also appears in the festivities associated with Twelfth Night, the day on which society was inverted – at the commencement of the day's festivities a cake containing a bean was cut, and whoever found the bean ruled the feast (a sort of Lord of Misrule) until midnight.

In Britain broad bean cultivation dates to at least the mid-6th century BC, with evidence in the form of seeds discovered on Iron Age sites. The literary record begins in the 10th century with *beana* in the *Læcboc of Bald* and *Greate beane* in the *Lacnunga*. An indication of its importance is the fact that the bean is the one vegetable set down in the Westminster Abbey Customary of 1270, a list of staples for which the monk-gardener was responsible. The other essentials are apples, cherries, pears, nuts and medlars. Neckam mentions broad beans in the 13th century and Parkinson in the early 17th century notes that they are extensively planted as a field crop and are a staple food of the poor, describing how they are 'boyled in faire water and a little salt, and afterwards stewed with some butter, a little vinegar and pepper being put unto them, and so eaten'.

Today broad beans are generally divided into three groups: Dwarf, Windsor and Longpod. There are a number of heritage varieties available, including an interesting rediscovery. In 1978 the cultivar 'Crimson-flowered' was saved from extinction when an elderly Miss Cutbush from Kent gave her last four seeds to the Heritage Seed Library. A 'Crimson Flour'd' was in cultivation by 1771 and described by Mawe in the 11th edition of *Every Man his own Gardener* (1787). Older still is 'Green Windsor', which appears under the name 'Toker' in the 1754 edition of Philip Miller's famous *The Gardeners Dictionary*: 'This sort bears the same relation to the Common Windsor that the Green does to the White Long-pod, except it ripens about the same time, or a few days later. It has the advantage of retaining its green colour when ripe'. However, its origin is probably of a much earlier date. More recent are 'Bunyard's Exhibition', which appeared in 1884 but is a synonym of 'Johnson's Wonderful Longpod'. *The Agriculturist's Manual* lists this as being offered by Lawson's Seed & Nursery Co. Ltd in 1836 as plain 'Johnson's Wonderful' and it is described as a 'newly introduced, and apparently a superior variety'. From the famous seed house of that name 'The Sutton Dwarf' was introduced in 1923 as 'A dwarf type, attaining a height of 9 to 12 ins. only when grown in the open ground'.

OPPOSITE *Broad beans 'Crimson-flowered', 'The Sutton Dwarf', 'Green Windsor', Bunyard's Exhibition' (left to right).* OVERLEAF *Broad beans 'The Sutton Dwarf', 'Crimson-flowered', 'Bunyard's Exhibition', 'Green Windsor' (left to right).*

BEANS

FRENCH OR KIDNEY BEAN
Phaseolus vulgaris

The wild strain of the French and runner bean is indigenous to the eastern slopes of the Andes and Mexico. Domestication occurred around the 6th millennium BC both in the Tehuacan Valley of Mexico and Callejon de Huaylas in Peru. Similar to those other famous introductions from the New World, the potato and tomato, the French bean is now a very varied vegetable, with an estimated 200 to 400 varieties and cultivars. They have a great variety of names, including common, green, French, borlotti (roman), haricot or navy (of baked beans fame), kidney, pinto and snap, and come in a range of different colours of pods and seeds, such as black, pink, red, white, green, yellow and mottled, and they may be either round or flat.

The bean was probably brought back by Columbus in 1493 and was certainly introduced by the Conquistadors, but its spread through Europe seems to have been via Italy in the 16th century. The French developed it, especially lower growing bush forms, hence one of its common names. Interestingly, descriptions and illustrations in the early literature reveal that both the climbing or pole and dwarf or bush forms were introduced to Europe contemporaneously. The earliest depiction of the dwarf form being in Fuchs in 1542 and the climbing form is found in *De Stirpium* by Hieronymus Tragus (or Jerome Bock; 1498–1554) a decade later.

The first mention of this bean in an English text is by Turner in 1548, when he gives three names: 'welshe Bonen', 'kidney bean' (on account of the bean's shape) and 'in frenche as some wryte Phaseole'. Barnaby Googe, the pastoral poet, also speaks of 'French beans' in 1572. In his famous *Herball* (1597) Gerard mentions four types of pole bean: the white, black, red and yellow, but does not mention the bush form. Parkinson in 1629 says that what he calls 'French or Kidney' beans 'are a dish more oftentimes at rich mens Tables than at the poore'. Only towards the end of the century, in 1683, did Worlidge state that 'within the memory of man the bean has from being a great rarity become a common delicate food'.

As mentioned, there are hundreds of varieties, but ones that can still be grown include 'Dutch Caseknife' (syn. 'Soissons Gros Blanc à Rames' listed in 1749) and 'Soldier', which is pre-1800. Dwarf bean 'Black Canterbury' has attractive black seeds.

OPPOSITE: ABOVE *French beans 'Soldier'*; BELOW LEFT *'Dutch Caseknife'*; BELOW RIGHT *'Black Canterbury'*.

It will thrive well in the City, the Smoke of
the Sea-coal being less injurious to this Plant
than most others … and, being supported
either with Sticks or Strings, grows up
to a good Height.

Miller, 1754

BEANS

SCARLET RUNNER BEAN
Phaseolus coccineus

Also a member of the *Phaseolus* genus and from the mountains of Central America, where it grows in cool, shady places, is the scarlet runner bean. With its (usually) bright red flowers and multi-hued seeds in shades of pink through to black, it is one of the most ornamental of all vegetables and was originally cultivated as such. It appears in the 1633 enlarged and posthumously published edition of Gerard's *Herball* edited by Thomas Johnson, where it is reported both that it 'was procured by Mr Tradescant' and that its flowers are 'large, many and of an elegant Scarlet colour'. But the first mention of it as a vegetable is made by Benjamin Townsend in *The Complete Seedsman* (1726), who says 'the cods are eaten sometimes, like other Kidney Beans'. In the 1754 edition of his *The Gardener's Dictionary*, Philip Miller calls it the Scarlet Bean and says it 'is very common in the English gardens, being planted for the Beauty of its scarlet Flowers'. He also mentions that it is grown over seats and arbours. The starchy roots of the scarlet runner bean are still eaten in Central America and the subspecies *darwinianus* is known as the Botil bean in Mexico.

Surviving heritage varieties include 'Painted Lady', with attractive bi-coloured flowers of red and white – hence it is also known as York and Lancaster – which probably dates to the 1630s and is thought by some to be a sport of 'Scarlet Runner'. Two favourites from the 19th century that are still grown are 'The Czar' and 'Sutton's Prizewinner'. 'The Czar' (syn. 'Mammoth White Runner'), with white flowers, was introduced in 1888 by the nurseryman Thomas Laxton of Bedford and was advertised as 'Useful in areas where flowers are eaten by birds who favour the white flowers less'. Introduced in 1882, 'Sutton's Prizewinner' is 'A long, straight, handsome Bean of table quality, the seed is quite distinct from all others'. From the 20th century 'Carter's Scarlet Emperor' was renamed by the seed house in 1906 from 'Mammoth Exhibition' and is now considered synonymous with the traditional 'Scarlet Runner'.

OPPOSITE: ABOVE *Scarlet runner beans 'The Czar'*; BELOW LEFT *'Painted Lady'*;
BELOW RIGHT *'Scarlet Emperor'*.

The Roots of the Red Beet, pared into thin Slices and Circles,
are by the French and Italians contriv'd into curious
Figures to adorn their Sallets.

Evelyn, 1699

BEETROOT
Beta vulgaris

The wild sea beet, *Beta vulgaris* subsp. *maritima*, native from Britain to Asia, is believed to be the ancestor of all cultivated beets. Domestication may have occurred in the Mediterranean, and although its cultivation is not mentioned by Classical authors, Apicius offers a recipe for cooking the beet root with honey. Beetroot, as distinct from the various forms of leaf beet (which were mentioned by many early authors and include chard, see p. 168), was not widely written about nor consumed during the medieval period. Moreover, the early beetroot did not look like the vegetable we are familiar with today, being carrot-shaped and described by Fuchs in his *De Historia Stirpium* (1542) as a 'single, long, straight, fleshy, sweet root'.

A few years later, in 1558, Matthiolus in his *Commentarii* notes that the Germans were cultivating 'a red beet with a swollen turnip-like root which is eaten'. This is the proto-beetroot and reveals that our beetroot is a relatively modern vegetable. In 1576, Matthias de L'Obel (1538–1616) published an illustration in his *Stirpium Observationes* (also shown by Henry Lyte in 1578), which reveals the first improvement to this red beet – the swollen root section is now wider than the collar. The name 'Roman beet', also used Gerard in 1597, may suggest Italian origins for the development of the modern beetroot. Parkinson in 1629 also describes the 'Romane red beet', mentioning both its shape – either short like a turnip or long like a carrot – and colour, being 'exceeding red'. By the mid-18th century the red beetroot was firmly established in the kitchen garden, and because of its strong colour became particularly fashionable in Victorian times. In the early 20th century the phrase 'take favours in the beetroot fields' was a popular euphemism for visiting prostitutes.

Of the surviving heritage varieties 'Cylindra' (syn. 'Formanova') dates back to the 1880s and has a long, slim root with dark red skin and flesh. The root grows above ground for easy lifting, is ideal for slicing and is sweet tasting. Dating to 1892 'Detroit Dark Red' produces deep red round roots, 8 cm (3 in.) in diameter, that have a fine texture and sweet flavour. The leaves ('tops') when small make an excellent spinach substitute in salads. Also pre-1900 is 'Bull's Blood', which may be a synonym for either 'Blood Red Hamburgh', in cultivation by 1878, or 'Dells Dark Crimson Dwarf Beet' that appeared in 1885. Both the leaves and the roots are eaten, the latter distinguished by their dark red colour; it is also an attractive addition to the flower garden.

Not all beetroots are red: for those wanting something different 'Burpee's Golden' (syn. 'Golden Detroit') dates to before 1806 and produces a golden yellow root, 'Chioggia' is an old Italian variety (1840s) with rings of white and red flesh, and there are also white cultivars, including 'Albina Vereduna' and from Holland 'Albino'.

OPPOSITE: ABOVE *Beetroot 'Bull's Blood'*; BELOW LEFT *beetroot 'Cylindra'*; BELOW RIGHT *beetroot 'Detroit Dark Red'*.

CARROT

Daucus carota

The garden carrot has a swollen, pigmented and sweet-tasting taproot; the native wild carrot (*Daucus carota*) has a white, spindly, bitter and tough root. For many centuries both were cultivated in the garden: the former as an edible vegetable and the latter for its seeds used in medicines. The domesticated carrot has a complex history, and it is not believed that the edible subspecies evolved from the wild form, for if left for a few generations the edible carrot will revert to something very different from the wild carrot. The root of the carrot has not survived in the archaeological record, but it is thought that an edible carrot with a purple root was domesticated in Afghanistan some 5,000 years ago. From here the carrot spread west and was known to ancient writers.

However, there has always been much academic discussion and general confusion concerning the carrot and the parsnip in Classical literary sources, because the authors are not always clear about exactly which vegetable is being discussed – the wild or cultivated form of carrot, or the parsnip. For example, in the Greek sources we find three words that could refer to the carrot and/or the parsnip: *sisaron*, which first appears in the writings of the dramatist and comic poet Epicharmus in around 500 BC; *staphylinos* is found in 430 BC in Hippocrates; and in the 1st century AD Dioscorides has *elaphoboscon*. The Roman Pliny, also in the 1st century AD, adds to the general confusion by interchanging *pastinaca*, *daucus*, and *sicer* or *siserum*.

A recent botanico-literary assessment by John Stolarczyk and Jules Janick (see Bibliography) has produced some clarification, concluding that early forms of carrot began to be cultivated in ancient Greece in the last few centuries BC and that the Greeks were aware of the carrot, wild carrot and parsnip. The Romans were certainly familiar with the cultivated carrot, and the first occurrence of the name *carotae* referring to the garden carrot is in the writings of Athenaeus in AD 200. By the 4th century the carrot was established in cultivation and Apicius offers four recipes in *De Re Coquinaria*.

The confusion begun by the ancients persisted. In the 16th century, for instance, Turner (1548) writes 'Pastinaca is called in Greek Staphilinos, in englishe a Carot', while the Sisaron 'is called in Englishe a Persnepe', and Daucus he considers to be 'Pastinaca sylvestris, in english wild carot'. Six years later, under *Staphylinos* Matthiolus talks about three plants: *Pastinaca domestica* (the modern parsnip), *P. sylvestris* (the wild carrot) and *Carota* (the cultivated carrot).

An examination of the archaeological record reveals that carrot seed is found in prehistoric Swiss lake dwellings in Robenhausen. Although it is not possible to distinguish between seed of the wild and domesticated forms, the absence of evidence of cultivation at the site suggests the medicinal use of harvested wild carrot seed. In Britain there is no specific evidence that the Romans introduced the cultivated carrot, but its marked increase in the archaeobotanical record over time strongly suggests this. If so, this would push back the date of Roman cultivation of the edible carrot to as early as the 1st century AD. In the late 8th century Charlemagne had carrots (and parsnips) included in *Capitulare de Villis* as one of the plants recommended for cultivation in his empire, and Albertus Magnus in his *De Vegetabilis et Plantis* (c. 1260) mentions that carrots were cultivated in the fields, orchards, gardens and vineyards of what is now Germany and France.

OPPOSITE *Carrots 'Long Red Surrey', 'Chantenay Red Cored' and 'St Valery'.*

The roote is round and long, thicke above
and small below, eyther red or yellow,
eyther shorter or longer.

Parkinson, 1629

By the 15th century an early orange cultivar had arrived in England, introduced by Flemish refugees and grown in Kent and Surrey. The carrot's status rose during the reign of Elizabeth I, with one legend describing how a courtier presented the queen with a tub of butter and a bunch of tender carrots emblazoned with diamonds; the diamonds were removed and the queen sent the carrots and butter to the kitchen, from where they returned as the now classic dish of buttered carrots.

In his *Herbull* (1597) Gerard writes that 'The root is long, thick and single, of a faire yellow colour, pleasant to be eaten, and very sweet in taste. There is another kind hereof like to the former in all parts, and differeth from it only in the colour of the root, which in this is not yellow, but of a blackish red colour.' Natural mutations of the purple-rooted form probably resulted in the red and yellow and subsequently orange forms, and it was the last that was selected and developed by plant breeders into the now familiar garden carrot. Exact dates cannot be established for the mutations, but while the process of active selection and development of the orange carrot took place in the 16th-century in Holland, the first illustration of a carrot of this colour dates as far back as AD 512 and a Byzantine edition of Dioscorides' *Codex Vindobonensis Medicus Graecus*.

Carrots, as with potatoes, are grouped according to sowing date and time taken for the root to mature. The general outdoor cropping groups are Early, Second Early, Maincrop and Late Crop. Sown between March and July a crop can be harvested from July until December; some can be stored over winter. Carrots may also be forced by using protected cropping (a glasshouse, cloches, horticultural fleece). Heritage varieties suitable for an early crop include 'Early Nantes', which dates to 1867 and is 'one of the earliest & best'; it has a cylindrical root 'with a blunt point,

even & clean; red, sweet & tender, coreless'. In cultivation by 1875 and 'The smallest & earliest carrot. Chiefly used for forcing' is 'Paris Market', which has a red root. A good range of orange-rooted Maincrop cultivars survive. Having orange roots with a distinctive yellow core and a fine flavour, 'Long Red Surrey' (syn. 'St. Valery', by 1821) was also named 'Chertsey' because of 'great quantities of it being brought to the markets of the metropolis from there'. The great French nurseryman Vilmorin described 'St Valery' in the 1856 edition of his *The Vegetable Garden* as 'A large handsome variety, with great productiveness, and at the same time a fine, regular shape, and thick, sweet, tender flesh'. Also dating to the 1820s and described by Vilmorin is 'Chantenay Red Cored' (by 1829); its 'roots are refined in appearance with small collars, evenly stumped with very small "tails" … Exterior colour rich orange'. From the 20th century a cultivar that is still popular is Carter's 'Autumn King 2' (*c.* 1900).

However, the wheel of garden fashion turns continually and we have now come full circle. For it is once again all the rage to grow 'novelty' cultivars with root colours other than orange. Carrot 'Black Spanish' (also known as 'Zanahoria Morada') is an Early purple cultivar which appears to have originated in the eastern Mediterranean or further east still, where it has been cultivated for over 300 years and is known as the 'Mulberry Carrot'. At the other end of the spectrum, dating to the 17th century and originating in Holland, 'White Belgium' (or 'Blanche') is white-rooted and of mild flavour. And somewhere in the middle lies the yellow-rooted 'Jaune Obtuse du Doubs' (syn. 'Yellow Intermediate', 1851), which is noted for its capacity for long winter storage.

OPPOSITE *Carrot 'Black Spanish'.*

CUCURBITS

The family Cucurbitaceae is known as the gourd family and is predominantly distributed within tropical zones around the world. Within its 125 genera are about 960 species, which include a number of annual vines grown as vegetables – the cucumber, melon (p. 190), squash and pumpkin (p. 170), which were among the first cultivated plants in both the Old and New Worlds.

CUCUMBER
Cucumis sativus

Archaeologists in Thailand have discovered evidence of cucumbers, which may have been semi-cultivated, dating from *c.* 9750 BC, and as a native of the foothills of the Himalaya, the cucumber has been cultivated in India for over 4,000 years. It must have from here that the plant was introduced to ancient Egypt and the eastern Mediterranean. Technically a creeping vine, the cucumber is listed among the food-stuffs of ancient Ur and was eaten in the *Epic of Gilgamesh*. Considered a most efficacious fruit, in the early 1st century AD doctors prescribed the Roman emperor Tiberius a cucumber a day. In order to maintain a supply for the patient, gardeners 'forced' cucumbers. Pliny describes a form of proto-glasshouse: 'raised beds made in frames upon wheels, by means of which the cucumbers were moved and exposed to the full heat of the sun; while, in winter, they were withdrawn, and placed under the protection of frames glazed with mirrorstone [mica]'.

The cucumber was a Roman introduction to the British Isles. In the *Læcboc of Bald*, *hwerhwette* is either cucumber or melon, and it certainly appears in Ælfric's *Glossary*. Roger, the gardener to the Archbishop of Canterbury at Lambeth Palace, purchased the seed of 'concomber & gourde' (the gourd is the bottle gourd or calabash) in 1321–22. Turner in 1548 names it the 'cucummer'. All of which goes to disprove Loudon's assertion in *Hortus Britannicus* (1830) that the cucumber was lost to cultivation and re-introduced in 1573. Samuel Pepys dramatically announces in his *Diary* for 22 August 1663 that 'Mr. Newburne … is dead of eating Cowcoumbers', a claim about as likely as success in the 'project for extracting sunbeams out of cucumbers' thought up by Jonathan Swift in his *Gulliver's Travels* (1726).

In medieval times cucumbers began to be cultivated on hotbeds, and in later centuries the bed was covered with glass-covered frames or 'lights', the direct descendants of those structures described by Pliny. From the 18th century onwards it was the fashion to grow cucumbers in glass-houses, the aim being to get the earliest crop possible. Equally important was the shape of the fruit. The engineer George Stephenson, of steam locomotive fame, patented the cucumber glass – a cylinder into which the developing fruit was inserted to ensure it grew straight. By the mid-19th century Cucumber Clubs had been established and were holding fiercely contested competitions. One of the most successful growers and breeders was James Barnes, later head gardener at Bicton in Devon, who raised 'Man of Kent'. Cucumber 'Crystal Apple' (syn. 'Crystal Lemon') was in cultivation in Britain by 1894 and is said to have originated in China. The smallish fruits have a pale lemon-coloured skin and are round, but taste exactly the same as the ordinary long green cucumber. Cucumber 'Tanja' is a European open-pollinated slicing cultivar producing long, firm, non-bitter fruits that harvest over a long period. Both the latter may be grown outdoors or in a greenhouse.

OPPOSITE: ABOVE & BELOW LEFT *Cucumber 'Tanja'*; BELOW RIGHT *cucumber 'Crystal Apple'.*

The … vegetable marrow, is that of all others most cultivated in gardens, and is a profitable and wholesome vegetable. It is used for culinary purposes in all stages of its growth, dressed either whole while quite young, or cut into sections as it gets larger.

M'Intosh, 1855

CUCURBITS

MARROW & COURGETTE

Cucurbita pepo

The courgette and zucchini are one and the same: the former name is derived from French, the latter from Italian, and both mean 'little marrow'. Indeed the marrow and courgette, together with certain pumpkins and squash (see p. 170), are botanically all varieties of the same species, which is native to Mesoamerica. Archaeological remains from the Guilá Naquitz cave, in the eastern range of mountains in the Valley of Oaxaca in Mexico, reveal that *Cucurbita pepo* was in domestication as early as 10,000 years ago, which predates the other great domesticates of the Americas, including maize and beans. This vegetable made the reverse journey to the cucumber, which was brought to the New World by Columbus, appearing in the Old World soon after the first contact.

The marrow, which is basically a courgette that has been allowed to develop to mature size (though there are different cultivars), has been grown in Europe since it was introduced in the 16th century. The cultivar 'Long Green Trailing' was in cultivation by 1879 and has tasty white flesh; it is robust, large and ornamental, with its dark and pale green stripes forming a striking contrast to other cultivars.

The courgette, however, owes a lot to 20th-century development, often the result of hybridization conducted in Italy, the offspring then being exported to North America by migrants in the 1920s. There are currently over 100 cultivars of courgette on the market, in an incredible range of colours, shapes and sizes – including the usual cigar shape and spherical, in shades of green, ivory white and the very popular yellow, with stripes, ridges, bumps and mottles. The golden zucchini, such as 'Burpee Golden', is an even more recent arrival, introduced in 1973 by the plant breeder Oved Shifriss (who also raised the 'Big Boy' tomato). Courgette 'Black Beauty Dark Fog' is of Italian origin, early maturing and produces dark blackish-green, glossy, firm but tender fruits over a long period; it was introduced into the United States in 1920. Another Italian heritage variety is 'Cocozelle', with attractive striped fruits and large flowers, which, like those of other courgettes, are also edible.

OPPOSITE *Courgette 'Cocozelle'*.

The fennel is beyond every other vegetable, delicious.
It greatly resembles in appearance the largest size celery,
perfectly white, and there is no vegetable equals it in flavor.
It is eaten at dessert, crude… Indeed I preferred it to
every other vegetable or to any fruit.

Thomas Appleton, 1824

FLORENCE FENNEL

Foeniculum vulgare var. *azoricum*

The word fennel evolved from the Latin *feniculum* meaning 'hay' via the Middle English *fenel* or *fenyl*. In ancient Greek the word for fennel is *marathon*, indicating that the place where the famous battle was fought in 490 BC was 'the place of fennel'. In Greek mythology a fennel stalk was used by Prometheus to steal fire from the gods and give it to mankind. It is likely that this was in fact a stalk of the giant fennel (*Ferula communis*), which was also used as the shaft of the *thyrsus* carried by Dionysos and his followers.

The species fennel is an aromatic and flavoursome herb with both culinary and medicinal uses. Florence fennel, Azorean fennel or finocchio, on the other hand, was selected and bred for its bulb-like, aniseed-flavoured swollen stem base, and was first widely cultivated in Italy. Absent from literature until the French author Johann Bauhin includes it in his *Historia plantarum universalis* (1651), Florence fennel appears to be a relative late-comer to the garden. The first British reference is 1728 and Stephen Switzer's snappily titled *A Compendious Method for the Raising of the Italian Brocoli, Spanish Cardoon, Celeriac, Finochi, and Other Foreign Kitchen Vegetables*, in which he notes that the 'Italian fennel' is recently introduced. Philip Miller discusses it in the 8th edition of his *The Gardener's Dictionary* (1758), saying this type of fennel came from the 'Azorian Islands' and had long been cultivated in Italy, where it was called 'finochio'. He admits, however, that 'there are not many English palates which relish it'. Not long after, Henry Stevenson in his *The gentleman gard'ner instructed, etc.* (7th ed., 1766) states that the vegetable is still rare in garden cultivation. In 1824 Thomas Jefferson was sent seeds of fennel from Italy by his friend and the consul in Leghorn (Livorno), Thomas Appleton, with a warm recommendation (quoted above). And it is a vegetable whose star is now on the rise.

OPPOSITE *Florence fennel.*

GLOBE ARTICHOKE & CARDOON

Cynara cardunculus Scolymus Group & *Cynara cardunculus*

The globe artichoke is cultivated for its large immature inflorescences, called capitula or heads. The edible parts are the fleshy lower portions of the bracts that make up the outer scales of the immature flower bud, and the base, known as the heart. If the buds are left to develop the resulting flower is a thistle-like rosette of a beautiful electric-blue colour. The common name artichoke is believed to derive from one of two northern Italian words: either *articoclos*, derived from *cocali*, the Ligurian word for pine cone, or *articiocco* which is derived from *al-kharshof*, the Arabic name for the plant. This perennial is a member of the family Asteraceae (sunflower) and indigenous to the Mediterranean region of southern Europe and North Africa.

Whether the artichoke in our sense was known to the Classical world continues to be debated because the literary sources are vague. The ancient Greek word often interpreted to mean artichoke is *skolymos*, which may also refer to other types of thistles, including the golden thistle (*Scolymus hispanicus*). Pliny discusses a plant that he says the Greeks call *scolymos*. Subsequent historical information is, however, scant. The Neapolitans cultivated the artichoke in the 9th century and it was spread by the Arabs during the early Middle Ages. Catherine de Medici, who married King Henry II of France in 1531, was reportedly very fond of the artichoke and took it with her to her new homeland. However, the artichoke must have also travelled north earlier and by an alternative route, for it was in cultivation in King Henry VIII's garden at New Hall in Essex by 1530, introduced into England by the Dutch. The artichoke quickly became a royal favourite in England, the king consuming 'generous quantities', perhaps because of the belief that it could enhance sexual prowess. Turner (1548) makes reference to both a wild (Carduus) and a garden form (Cinara) of 'Archichoke', which could be a distinction between the cardoon and artichoke. However, he does not state if both are cultivated, and half a century later Gerard, that collector of novelty, was growing the latter but not the former.

While a popular vegetable, the artichoke was not subjected to intensive breeding. Parkinson describes seven sorts in 1629, and a century later Miller (1731) has only one sort growing around London. By the mid-19th century M'Intosh in *The Book of the Garden* (1855) could only recommend five cultivars. However, several heritage varieties have survived from the 18th century. The French cultivar 'Gros Vert de Lâon' (syn. 'Large Green Paris', by 1756) is considered to be one of the finest flavoured of all artichokes. Although not early maturing and suitable only for warmer areas, it does produce a consistently high yield. Originating in Brittany, 'Camus' (syn. 'Camus de Bretagne') is a deep ash-green artichoke with a tender succulent heart and a rounded, compact and large head. Indeed 'Camus' is generally considered to be the largest cultivar, with the heads up to 500 g (18 oz) in weight. Other heritage varieties still available include 'Green Globe' (by 1791) and 'Purple Globe (syn. 'Romanesco', by 1835).

The edible part of the cardoon, a plant which closely resembles the artichoke, is the stem, which is blanched and tastes like a cross between artichoke and asparagus. The cardoon derives its name from the Latin *carduus* or thistle, referring to its spininess. It is mentioned by Ruellius in his *De natura stirpium libri tres* (1536) and by Matthiolus in his *Commentarii* (1554), and the plant features in the still lifes of Juan Sánchez Cotán in the early 17th century. Parkinson (1629) discusses the 'chardon', stating that John Tradescant had told him that three acres of land around Brussels was planted with the chardon and that it was 'white'ed like Endiue' (i.e. blanched). John Tradescant the Elder travelled to the Low Countries between 1610 and 1611 at the behest of his employer, the 1st Earl of Salisbury, with instructions to collect novelties for his new garden at Hatfield House, and thus it is possible that it was he who introduced the cardoon to England around this date.

OPPOSITE *Globe artichokes 'Camus' and 'Gros Vert de Lâon'.*

Pease are of divers kinds … the meaner sort of them have been long acquainted with our English Air and Soil; but the sweet and delicate sorts of them have been introduced into our Gardens only in this latter age.

Worlidge, 1683

PEA

Pisum sativum

A century and a half ago the pea played a significant role in the science of genetics when the Austrian monk Gregor Mendel used it the 1860s in his studies into the transfer of character traits between generations, thus establishing the basic tenets of genetic inheritance. Sadly, Mendel and his pioneering findings were ignored during his lifetime and it was not until 1900, when the Dutch botanist Hugo de Vries rediscovered his work, that Mendel received the recognition he was due. This may be seen as an appropriate honour for one of the first crops to be domesticated.

The pea is an annual climber which produces a podded fruit. Within individual seed pods are a number of small spherical seeds – the peas – which can be used either fresh or dried. The wild pea is native to the Mediterranean basin and the Near East. The oldest peas in the archaeological record date to the Neolithic age and have been discovered in Syria, Turkey and Jordan, and the pea was also grown from ancient times in Egypt. From these two regions the pea moved east, to Afghanistan by *c.* 2000 BC, and then onwards through Pakistan reaching the Gangetic basin and southern India by the second half of the 2nd millennium BC. And it also spread north into Europe: the pea was known to the Greek and Roman authors, though the scarcity of their writings suggests it was not widely cultivated, perhaps because it is a cool season crop. But cultivated it was, for in the 4th century Apicius offers nine recipes for cooking peas.

The word pea, in old English texts 'pease', is derived from the Latin *pisum*, which in turn comes from the Greek, *pison*, though the pea was not introduced to Britain by the Romans since it was already present. Peas have been found at the Early Iron Age site at Glastonbury in Somerset dating to the 6th century BC. In the Middle Ages, the pea, like that other staple pulse, the broad bean (see p. 84), was grown predominantly as a field crop. Ruellius (1536) makes the first specific reference to a garden pea – a climbing pea whose fresh pods and their peas were eaten. Gerard also mentions it, yet in England the garden pea remained a rarity in Tudor gardens. Early in the reign of Elizabeth I fresh peas were imported from Holland and were 'fit dainties for ladies, they came so far and cost so dear'.

A century later Leonard Meager, in the 2nd edition of his *The English Gardener* (1683), names nine kinds of pea in cultivation (200 years later Vilmorin describes 149), and in the same year Worlidge notes the introduction of 'sugar pease'. Thus it appears that the garden pea is a 17th-century introduction to Britain from the Low Countries, perhaps via France. The petit pois may have a different origin, for legend has it that in 1533 Catherine de Medici (see also p. 105) brought to France a small, sweet pea known in her homeland as *piselli novelli*.

Snap (or sugarsnap) and snow peas are different varieties of pea, the pods of which are consumed together with their contents. The snap peas (*Pisum sativum* var. *macrocarpon*) have a round pod, the snow peas (*Pisum sativum* var. *saccharatum*) a flat pod. The name mangetout is today applied generally to both snap and snow peas, and one form of 'eat all' pea was certainly in cultivation by 1855, when it was mentioned by M'Intosh.

Peas are another crop whose cultivars are grouped by sowing date and time to harvest. M'Intosh praises 'Prince Albert' (syn. 'Early Kent'), an Early cultivar that probably dates to before 1837, although the first advertisement for its commercial sale is in 1842. Cormack & Oliver, Seedsmen & Nurserymen of New Cross in London, boasted that in a trial, seed planted on 14 March was harvested on 25 April. Another Early pea is 'Veitch's Western Express', which was bred by that nursery company and is particularly useful in a coastal location. Maincrop types 'Magnum Ne Plus Ultra' (before 1847) and 'Magnum Bonum' (*c.* 1860) are among the tallest of the available heritage varieties, readily reaching 2.1 m (7 ft). And named to honour the four times British Prime Minister, 'Gladstone' was raised by a grower called Mr Holmes before 1896. It produces a deliciously sweet pea and is resistant to drought.

And just for the record, the asparagus pea (*Psophocarpus tetragonolobus*) is not a pea, nor is it a winged bean (another common name), but is a tropical legume native to New Guinea. With a similar habit to a pea it has become a novelty vegetable in recent years.

OPPOSITE: ABOVE *Pea 'Prince Albert'*; BELOW LEFT *pea 'Magnum Ne Plus Ultra'*; BELOW RIGHT *pea 'Magnum Bonum'*. OVERLEAF *Pea 'Veitch's Western Express'*.

I do remember him at Clement's Inn, like a man made
after supper of a cheese-paring; when he was naked, he was,
for all the world, like a forked radish, with a head
fantastically carved upon it with a knife.

Shakespeare, *Henry IV, Part II*

RADISH
Raphanus sativus

The garden radish is a cool-season, fast-maturing vegetable which we most commonly cultivate for its small, red-skinned, white translucent-fleshed, peppery-tasting, round or cylindrical root, commonly enjoyed in late spring and summer. There are, however, also cultivars that are sown in the autumn for a winter harvest. These winter radishes grow considerably larger and usually have a stronger flavour. Yet it may come as a surprise to discover that the unprepossessing garden radish is but one of various forms grown around the world down the centuries, and not just for its root. For example, in 18th-century England the radish was cultivated for its leaves, which were consumed in salads, and in Asia and China certain cultivars are today grown for their edible pods and seeds, and for the oil that is extracted from the latter.

The name radish derives from *radix*, the Latin for root, and the genus name *Raphanus* is from the Greek meaning 'quickly appearing', referring to the seed's speedy germination. The species name *sativus*, often used for vegetables, just means sown from seed or cultivated. Both Greeks and Romans grew various kinds of radish. Herodotus refers to radishes (as well as onion and garlic) being fed to the workers constructing the pyramids in Egypt, so they must have been a staple there. A round form of radish was called *boeotion* by Theophrastus, and by Pliny and Columella the *syriacum*. What may be today's garden radish was the *radicula* of Columella and the *algidense* of Pliny. Further east, the radish was (and is) popular in both Japan and China. However, there are almost no archaeological records to shed light on the radish's earliest domestication. Wild species are native across western Asia and Europe, including Britain, but exactly where and when the radish jumped the garden wall remains a mystery.

The cultivated radish is among the plants listed in *Capitulare de Villis* at the end of the 8th century and is named in both in the *Læcboc of*

Bald and the *Lacnunga* as the *ontre* and *rædic*. The first northern European account of radish cultivation appears in the 13th century, when Albertus Magnus describes the *radix* as a large, long and white root of 'a pyramidal figure [and] a somewhat sharp savor' that was harvested in the winter; so perhaps the winter radish predates the summer one. Three hundred years later Turner, in *The Names of Herbes* (1548), states that the 'radix' or 'commune radice or radishe wyth the longe roote … groweth communely in England'. Lyte in *A Niewe Herball* (1578) confirms this, adding that a similar type but with a black root had recently arrived in England and was becoming popular. Gerard (1597) also names a 'Blacke radish' and 'Round rooted blacke Radish'. The former may be the still available 'Black Spanish Long', and the latter perhaps 'Black Spanish Round'.

Of the other heritage cultivars that remain in cultivation 'White Icicle' (syn. 'The Long White', 'White Italian' and 'Naples Radish') is a spring cultivar with a long root. 'Rat-tailed' (by 1867) is grown for its edible seed pods. Of the red radishes 'Scarlet Globe' (by 1881) is still a great favourite, producing scarlet, globed-shaped roots, and 'French Breakfast' (syn. 'Flamboyant', 1865) is a solid, sweet, cylindrical radish that sports crimson shoulders and a white tip and is considered good for forcing and producing an early crop. 'D'Avignon', as the name suggests, originates from the south of France and produces elongated red radishes with a white tip in just three weeks, while 'Sparkler' (by 1885) is a summer radish producing round, red-skinned roots with a white splash at the root end.

OPPOSITE *Radishes 'Scarlet Globe', 'National', 'D'Avignon', 'White Breakfast' and 'Sparkler' (left to right).*

RHUBARB
Rheum × hybridum

The genus *Rheum* contains 60 or so species and is native to the mountains of western and northwestern China, India, Tibet, Russia and Turkey. The edible rhubarb is an attractive herbaceous perennial, with large leaves (which are poisonous) supported on long fleshy pink-tinged and triangular-shaped stalks (technically petioles but called sticks), which are the part we eat. But rhubarb was first cultivated in China not as an ingredient for a tasty crumble, but for the medicinal properties of its root, a use to which it has been put since about 2700 BC.

The name *Rheum* might be related to the vegetable's purgative quality, derived from *rheo*, the Greek 'to flow'. Alternatively it may be the plant Dioscorides called *rha* or *rheon*, which was found around the Bosphorus. Pliny discusses a plant called 'rhacoma', which may be rhubarb, and the late Roman historian Ammianus Marcellinus (4th century AD) mentions that on the banks of the river *Rha*, today called the Volga, grew a plant of the same name, which is generally regarded as rhubarb. This could also be the origin of 'rhubarb' – a derivation from the Latin *Rha barbarum*, meaning something like 'foreign stuff from the Volga'.

From the literary sources of the 17th and 18th centuries it appears that rhubarb was a late arrival in the garden, but exactly how it got here is a mystery. It is believed that *R. rhaponticum* was introduced into Europe in around 1608 and was subsequently cultivated by Alpinus in the Botanic Garden in Padua before travelling north. The date that rhubarb arrived in England is uncertain, but in 1777 *Rheum rhaponticum* was planted by Hayward, an apothecary of Banbury in Oxfordshire, and his plants may be the ancestors of today's rhubarb fields.

The first mention of rhubarb being eaten appears a year later, when Mawe notes that the 'young stalks in spring, being cut and peeled, are used for tarts'. As the various species of *Rheum* arrived in Britain they were all tested for edibility. *Rheum palmatum* (Chinese Rhubarb) was cultivated in Edinburgh by 1762, and *Rheum hybridum* arrived in England in 1773 or 1774. The latter did not become a culinary plant until the 1820s. The ancestry of what is now widely grown as English rhubarb – *Rheum × hybridum* (syn. *R. × cultorum*) is confused, although one parent is believed to be *R. rhaponticum*.

Rhubarb can be grown outdoors, when tall rhubarb pots are used to force the crop, or indoors in darkened sheds. It is from these sheds in the 'rhubarb triangle' of West Yorkshire that the season's first stems are cut, traditionally by candlelight. In 2010 Yorkshire Forced Rhubarb was awarded Protected Designation of Origin status by the European Union. And as to whether rhubarb is a vegetable or a fruit, it is generally considered a vegetable, but in 1947 a court in Buffalo, New York, decided that because rhubarb was used as a fruit it was to be counted as such for the purposes of regulations and duties, a ruling that reduced taxes paid.

Of the heritage varieties still available 'Timperley Early' has a superb flavour, produces long sticks and is a very early variety good for forcing. Also cropping early is 'Hawkes' Champagne', which produces especially sweet sticks. 'Myatt's Victoria' was introduced by the nursery company J. & W. Myatt by 1837, with seedlings costing 10s per 100, and is still an excellent rhubarb, while 'Reed's Early Superb' (syn. 'Fenton's Special') is, despite the name, a mid-season variety of rhubarb that produces very deep red sticks; it also forces well.

OPPOSITE *Rhubarb 'Reed's Early Superb' and (on right) 'Timperley Early' (forced).*

SALADS

Salad is a general term covering numerous different types of leafy green vegetables, often mixed together and usually eaten raw. The precise ingredients have varied over time and from place to place, depending on what was grown and what was in fashion. In 1699 John Evelyn devoted a treatise to the subject: Acetaria: A Discourse of Sallets.

LETTUCE
Lactuca sativa

The lettuce is perhaps the most commonly consumed of all salad leaves. The name 'lettuce' is derived from the Old French word 'laitues', while the genus name *Lactuca* is from the Latin *lac*, meaning 'milk', a reference to the milky sap produced when a lettuce stem is cut. Cultivated salad lettuces are likely descendants of the wild prickly lettuce (*Lactuca serriola*), which has very bitter leaves and a wide distribution. Prickly lettuce is shown in ancient Egyptian tomb paintings and was sacred to Min, the priapic god of fertility, as it was believed to possess aphrodisiacal qualities.

Herodotus recounts in his *The Histories* that the lettuce was served at the dining table of the Persian kings, while Hippocrates ascribed medicinal properties to it, believing that it induced sleep. This somnolent effect was also referred to by Beatrix Potter in *The Tale of the Flopsy Bunnies*. Pliny described nine types of lettuce in cultivation by the 1st century, and it became 'Cos' (the alternative name for the 'Romaine') because it was discovered on the Greek Island of Kos and renamed by the Romans. The Romans introduced the salad lettuce into northern and western Europe, including Britain, and it is well represented in medieval sources. Turner (1548) names it the 'lettis', and Gerard gives good cultivation advice in 1597, stating that the lettuce 'delighteth to grow … in a manured, fat, moist, and dunged grounde'.

Lettuces are divided into types based on their leaf and head qualities. Butterhead types form a loose head with leaves of a buttery texture. Looseleaf types have open, floppy heads, with tender and mildly flavoured leaves, and include oakleaf and lollo rosso. Romaine or Cos types produce a tall conical head of sturdy leaves with a firm midrib. The crisphead or

Iceberg lettuce was introduced in the 1930s and forms a tight, dense head resembling a cabbage. In the days before refrigerated transportation, Californian growers piled crushed ice on top of the lettuces which then looked like green icebergs, hence the name.

Fashionable once again are spotted and red-leaved cultivars, but they are no recent creation: red-spotted forms of Romaine were in cultivation by 1623. Thankfully, a wealth of heritage varieties is still available, some of the oldest being French. 'Blonde de Paris' (syn. 'Batavia Blonde' or 'White Silesian') was in cultivation by 1751, and 'Verte Maraîchère' (syn. 'Green Paris Cos') by 1771. 'Green Oakleaf' also dates to 1771, and with similar oakleaf-shaped leaves but of a striking rich red colour 'Red Oakleaf' dates to the 19th century. The perennially popular early maturing 'Tom Thumb' (syn. 'Stone Tennisball') was in cultivation by 1784. A 19th-century cultivar, 'Winter Density', with dark green leaves and tightly folded heads, is both very winter hardy and heat tolerant. Introduced in 1850, 'Marvel of Four Seasons' is a butterhead from France, where it is known as 'Merveille de Quatre Saisons'; the colour of the splotched reddish green rosette intensifies with cool weather, and it has excellent flavour. 'Little Gem' (syn. 'Sucrine'), once again in commercial cultivation, dates from 1880. The curiously named 'Drunken Woman' (syn. 'Ubriacona Frastagliata') is an old Italian looseleaf cultivar that has frilly leaves with an attractive reddish margin and good flavour. Also for the misogynist, 'Fat Lazy Blonde' (syn. 'Grosse Blonde Paresseuse') was in cultivation by 1856.

OPPOSITE *Lettuces 'Green Oakleaf' and 'Red Oakleaf' (in basket), and 'Drunken Woman'.*

Raw Purslane is much used in sallades, with oyle,
salt and vinegre: it cooleth an hot stomacke
and proveketh appetite.

Gerard, 1633

SALADS

ALEXANDERS & PURSLANE

Smyrnium olusatrum & *Portulaca oleracea*

Believed to be named after the Egyptian city of Alexandria from which it originated, Alexanders is written about by Theophrastus, Dioscorides, Columella and Pliny, who says it is also known as 'hipposelinum', or horse parsley, and smyrnium. It is also on Charlemagne's 'to plant' list. An attractive umbellifer with yellow-green flowers, it is a native of the Mediterranean and grows wild in Britain and elsewhere. In the 1633 edition of Gerard's *Herball* it is noted that 'the root hereof is also in our age served to the table raw for a sallad herbe'. Young shoots and leaves are eaten as salads and the stem like celery. However, by the late 18th century cultivation of Alexanders seems to have fallen from fashion, a situation that persists to this day, but it is an interesting and unusual addition to the summer salad bowl.

A native of North Africa and the Middle East, cultivated purslane differs from its wild form in that it has an erect rather than a prostrate habit. Greek and Roman writers referred to purslane as *andrachne* and *portulaca* respectively. However, purslane seems not to have been cultivated in northern Europe until the mid-16th century when Ruellius refers to both the erect and procumbent types, describing three forms of the latter: the green leaved, the golden leaved and the large golden leaved. Parkinson describes it in 1629, and it appears in the 1633 edition of Gerard's *Herball*. M'Intosh (1855) says of it that 'its young shoots and leaves, which are very fleshy or succulent, are used in summer salads, and sometimes used in French and Italian soups and also as pickles'. Tasting slightly sour and salty, it is another salad crop which has fallen from fashion but is worthy of cultivation.

OPPOSITE LEFT *Alexanders.* OPPOSITE RIGHT *Purslane.*

Spinach, Spinachia … being boil'd to a Pult, and without other
Water than its own moisture, is a most excellent Condiment
with Butter, Vinegar, or Limon, for almost all sorts of boil'd
Flesh … and (tho' by original a Spaniard) may be had
at almost any Season, and in all places.

Evelyn, 1699

SPINACH
Spinacia oleracea

Native to central and southwestern Asia this leafy vegetable, which seems to have been unknown to the Greeks and Romans, is thought to have been domesticated in Persia. There the first record of spinach cultivation is from the Sasanian civilization and dates to the 3rd century AD. From Persia spinach reached China by the mid-7th century and Sicily by 827, brought there by the Saracens. Moorish invaders took spinach to Andalusia, where in the 12th century Ibn al-'Awwam calls it 'the prince of vegetables'. Spinach is not mentioned in any European medieval texts until the *Liber Ruralium Commodorum* of Crescentiis in 1305, and it is not known how it first reached Britain – whether directly from Spain, or brought back from Sicily by a returning Crusader, or simply crossing the Channel from France.

The first English gardening reference to spinach is in Jon Gardener's *The Feate of gardening* (*c.* 1400), but a slightly earlier literary reference appears as *spinnedge* and *spynoches* in the first English cookery book, *The Forme of Cury* (1390). By 1530 the word 'spinach' was in use and may derive from the Andalusian Arabic *asbinakh* meaning 'green hand', via the French *espinache* – which may indicate that the introduction to Britain was from France. By the mid-16th century spinach was in cultivation across Europe, though in spite of the best efforts of Popeye it has always remained a vegetable of relatively minor popularity in Britain. The cultivar 'Bloomsdale Long-Standing' was in cultivation by 1887, when it was described as having 'Dark glossy green leaves crumpled & blistered. Vigorous, with tender fleshy leaves that have a rich flavour'.

New Zealand spinach (*Tetragonia tetragonioides*) is a native of Tasmania, Australia and South America, as well as New Zealand, and was discovered by Sir Joseph Banks. George Henslow in *The Origin and History of our Garden Vegetables* (1912) states that 'The leaves are thick and used as a substitute for spinach, but the mucilage in the leaves is somewhat objectionable'.

OPPOSITE *Spinach 'Bloomsdale Long-Standing'.*

TOMATO

Solanum lycopersicum

Technically a fruit, the tomato is native to South America, with its genetic 'hot spot' centred on the Andes of Peru, where eight species still grow in the wild. From here one species – *Solanum lycopersicum* – was transported north to Mexico and cultivated by Mesoamerican cultures. Our word 'tomato' relates to two Nahuatl words for 'swelling fruit' – *xitomatl* and *centtomati* – and evidence of its use as a decoration as well as a consumable dates to *c.* AD 700 and the Aztec empire. It was from Mexico that the tomato crossed the Atlantic – according to some it was with Columbus in 1493, though its absence from the literature of the early 16th century suggests a later date, sometime in the aftermath of Cortés's conquest of the Aztec capital of Tenochtítlan (Mexico City) in 1521. The earliest European literary reference is by Matthiolus in *Commentarii* (1554), in which he states that the tomato was recently arrived in Italy where it was called *pomi d'oro* (golden apple). This name perhaps reflects the prevalence of yellow-fruiting types, although Matthiolus also describes red fruit and other contemporary sources reveal the existence of a range of different coloured fruits – ochre, deep orange, purple red, versicoloured and white.

The first English reference to golden apples comes, with an illustration, in 1578 and Henry Lyte's *A Niewe Herball*. Lyte gives various names, including *Poma Amoris* and the French *pommes d'amour*. However, these are more likely a corruption of one or other of the early Italian or Spanish names – the latter being *pome dei Moro* or apple of the Moors – than a reference to any aphrodisiac quality. Both in England and on the continent the tomato was initially treated with great suspicion because of its resemblance to another member of the family Solanaceae, deadly nightshade. Some of the belladonna folklore associations with werewolves and witches rubbed off on to the tomato, and when Linneus came to classify it he named it *Lycopersicum esculentum*, meaning 'edible wolf peach', a reference to the German common name for the fruit. The potato (see p. 33) was also treated with scepticism after its arrival, but in the case of the tomato the prejudice lasted even longer. It is perhaps surprising given the tomato's ubiquitous position in most global cuisines today that it remained unpopular until the late 19th century; culinary use was limited to sauces. Indeed, in Britain it was not until after the First World War that the tomato began to be consumed in large quantities. This may be one reason why relatively few early cultivars remain available. Of those that do 'Yellow Currant' was in cultivation by 1795 while 'Yellow Pear' is older still, dating to the 17th century. From the 19th century the traditional French cultivar 'St Pierre' (syn. 'Saint Peter') was in cultivation by 1880, and 'Golden Sunrise' dates from 1888.

The tomato is another edible that has come under the scrutiny of the American legal system (see also rhubarb, p. 112), in this case the Supreme Court. In 1893 John Nix claimed that because the tomato is botanically a fruit and not a vegetable his imports should not be subjected to the Tariff Act. He lost. In fact many heirloom varieties of tomato remain available in the United States. Among the finest is 'Brandywine Yellow', which originated in Ohio and was in cultivation by 1884; it is a small yellow beefsteak tomato that matures early. A ribbed-shoulder tomato from West Virginia, the fruits of 'Striped German' can weigh upwards of 1 kg (over 2 lb) and are shaded yellow and red. Of a colour and shape as suggested by its name, 'Orange Strawberry' is of beefsteak size with great flavour; it was raised from a rogue seed in a packet of 'Pineapple' by a Mrs Morris of Indiana. 'Pink Ping Pong' produces amazing yields of dusky-rose pink fruits of appropriate size, juicy and bursting with superb flavours. Bred by Michael Byrne of Lawton in Michigan, 'Slankards' produces a high yield of large, meaty, semi-heartshaped fruit with great flavour. More historic still is an ancient variety from the Zapotec people of Oaxaca in Mexico: with mild tasting flesh, the fruits of 'Zapotec' have a distinctive fluted or ribbed form. Last, but far from least, 'Roma' is the deep red plum tomato familiar from supermarket shelves, which is ideal for salads, bottling, soups, sauces and sun drying. It was introduced in 1955 and is open-pollinated, but because it is commercially cultivated it is not generally considered a heritage cultivar – yet it is an all-round outstanding tomato and should not be excluded.

OPPOSITE *Tomatoes 'Roma' (in bowl) and 'St Pierre'.* OVERLEAF *Tomatoes 'Zapotec', 'Slankards' and 'Striped German' (left to right).*

Autumn

The fragrance of autumn is rich and mellow, redolent of bonfire smoke and the earthiness of fallen leaves, the yeasty smells of harvested fruits, and savours of chutneys and jams bubbling on the stove. The taste of autumn is the first apple from the tree, the crisp juicy flesh with its acid-sweet perfection. This is the season of long rays of soft golden light piercing chill, misty mornings and evenings, the fiery exuberance of Nature celebrating her work done, the pale blue skies painted over with vivid-hued sunsets. For all its brilliance autumn can be the most calm and reflective of seasons in the garden – harvests continue, but not at such a frenetic pace. It is time to slow down, to rake leaves, clear and dig beds, to prepare the soil for winter slumber.

AUTUMN FRUIT

APPLE
Malus domestica

Long has it been held that the domestic apple is descended from the European crab apple (*M. sylvestris*), but recent DNA analysis has established that the ancestor is in fact the wild species *M. sieversii*, indigenous to the mountains of Kazakhstan, Kyrgyzstan, Tajikistan, northern Afghanistan and Xinjiang, China. The apple, along with the pear and quince, is a pome fruit, consisting of a fleshy, enlarged receptacle (the part we eat) surrounding the tough core containing the seeds.

The first Western literary reference is found in *The Odyssey* (see p. 12), and according to Greek mythology it was the apple that, indirectly, sent Odysseus to Troy. When Paris judged Aphrodite more beautiful than Athena or Hera, awarding her a golden apple from the Garden of the Hesperides, his bribe and reward was Helen, thus sparking the Trojan War. Beauty aside, the apple was properly Hera's property because the tree that produced these immortality-giving apples, which stood in the Garden cared for by the nymphs of the evening and guarded by the serpent-dragon Ladon, had been a wedding gift to her and Zeus from Gaia. Another of these apples was stolen by Hercules in completion of his 11th Labour. The apple is similarly imbued with qualities of immortality in Norse mythology: the goddess Iðunn supplied gods with apples that provided eternal youth. And of course the apple is associated with the forbidden fruit of the Garden in Eden and the temptation of Adam by Eve. However, the apple is not specifically identified in the Book of Genesis and many consider the forbidden fruit to be the apricot (see p. 41). Similarly, Hera's 'apples' may have been quinces (see p. 165).

Pliny names 21 types of apple and it was the Romans who introduced the domesticated apple to England, since when it has never fallen from favour. There is even a possible surviving legacy. Said to have been brought by a General Ezio from Latium, the cultivar 'Decio'

offers an insight into how very early apples taste: 'firm, fine flesh with a slightly sweet, slightly subacid flavour', according to the National Fruit Collection description. The *æppel* is listed in *Læcboc of Bald*, and both the apple and crab apple (*wergule*) are in the *Lacnunga*. References to the apple appear in all other early and medieval texts, suggesting that it quickly became established as a popular fruit both in Britain and on the continent. The *pomerium* or utilitarian orchard was integral to the medieval monastic garden – one is clearly marked on the famous plan of Christ Church in Canterbury (*c.* 1165); and it is not unreasonable to assume that as new sister houses were established, so new cultivars were brought from the continent by the pioneering monks, and new cultivars raised. One monastic survivor is 'Melrose', thought to have originated in the Cistercian monastery of the Scottish town of that name.

The conquering Normans brought with them a tradition of ornamental gardening, and fruit trees were widely planted within the enclosed confines of the ornamental garden or *viridarium*. In 1280, the wife of King Edward I, queen Eleanor of Castile (see p. 15), planted 'Blandurel' (syn. 'Reinette Grise'), which originated in Poitou in France, in her garden at King's Langley. It is sadly no longer available, but other cultivars dating back to the Middle Ages have survived, including 'Pearmain' (syn. 'Winter Pearmain' and 'Old English Pearmain'), which was favoured as both a dessert and cider apple. Before 1204 the manor of Runham in Norfolk was held by 'petty sarjeanty', the yearly payment to the Exchequer being 200 Pearmains and four firkins of cider made from this apple. And if the

OPPOSITE: ABOVE *Apples 'D'Arcy Spice', 'Api Noir', 'Calville Blanc d'Hiver', 'Decio', 'Golden Knob';* BELOW LEFT *apple 'Flower of Kent';* BELOW RIGHT *apple 'Calville Rouge d'Automne'.*

*The best sorts of Apples serve at the last course for the table,
in most mens houses of account … Divers other sorts serve to bake,
either in pyes or pans, or else stewed in dishes with Rosewater
and Sugar, and Cinamon or Ginger cast upon.*

Parkinson, 1629

great 19th-century pomologist Robert Hogg is to be believed (in the 5th edition of his magisterial *The Fruit Manual*, 1884) the famous 'Costard', a cooking apple first recorded in 1296 and purveyed by Costermongers, is synonymous with the still available 'Catshead'. Another old survivor is 'Nonpareil', which is believed to be of French origin and introduced in the mid-16th century, perhaps as part of Henry VIII's drive to improve fruit growing and revive the orchard industry (see p. 16). The flesh is greenish-white, fine-textured and juicy, with a slightly acid and aromatic flavour.

Parkinson (1629) names 60 cultivars, dividing them by use: eating (dessert), cooking, for making cider and for the manufacture of a form of 'sweet oyntement' called Pomatum, much used to help 'chapt' skin. Several of Parkinson's recommendations remain in cultivation, for instance 'Golden Pippin', 'Rambures' (syn. 'Rambour Franc') and 'Carpendu' (syn. 'Court Pendu Gris'). But the most famous apple of the 17th century has to be the cooking apple 'Flower of Kent'. For in 1665 it was beneath a tree of this cultivar at Woolsthorpe Manor near Grantham in Lincolnshire that Sir Isaac Newton was sitting when an apple fell by him. The rest, as they say, is history. The cultivar dates to the 15th century and although Newton's tree blew down in a storm in 1820 it was propped up and continues to fruit to this day.

Apples were the subject of extensive hybridization in the 19th century, and the number of books dedicated to the apple and apple growing suggests its cultivation became something of a mania. The same century saw the appearance of a number of cultivars that continue to be widely consumed. On this criteria these commercial cultivars are technically excluded from heritage status, but only a pedant would reject such delicious fruits. The cooking apple 'Bramley's Seedling' was raised in Southwell in Nottinghamshire, between 1809 and 1813, but became commercially available only in 1876. The delicious 'Worcester Pearmain', possibly a seedling of 'Devonshire Quarrenden' (which itself was first recorded in 1678), came on the market in 1874 raised by a Mr Hall of Swan Pool near Worcester. Perhaps the most famous of all British apples, 'Cox's Orange Pippin' was raised by Richard Cox, a brewer who at the age of 45 retired to Colnbrook Lawn, Slough. Here he dedicated himself

to his passion of gardening and in around 1825 planted two seeds from a 'Ribston Pippin' (itself raised at Ribston Hall in Yorkshire from seed brought from Rouen *c.* 1707). One grew up to become 'Cox's Orange Pippin', the other 'Cox's Pomona'. Grafts were supplied to the nursery Messrs Smale and Sons at Colnbrook, who offered the first trees for sale in 1840. At the Great Apple Show organized by the RHS in 1883, of the 183 exhibitors of dessert apples 123 showed 'Cox's Orange Pippin'.

The apple is perhaps the fruit that offers the most choice when it comes to growing heritage varieties. 'Court Pendu Plat' is of European origin, and although dated to 1613 may be of Roman pedigree. With rich, aromatic fruit containing a good balance of sugar and acid, this is a cultivar useful in areas prone to late frosts. Introduced in 1670, the French cultivar 'Calville Rouge d'Automne' has a sweet, slightly strawberry flavour, with tender, juicy flesh and makes a great baked apple. With a strong flavour and recommended by the RHS as an excellent attractant and nectar source for bees and other beneficial insects, 'Court of Wick' originated in Somerset and dates to 1790. Notable for its spice-like flavour as the name suggests, 'D'Arcy Spice' can possibly be traced to the gardens of Tolleshunt D'Arcy Hall in Essex and dates to before 1800. It has good disease resistance, stores well and is tolerant of poor soils, though may crop variably each year. With its unusual knobbly skin and sweet, creamy flesh 'Knobbed Russet' (syn. 'Knobby Russet', 'Winter Russet' and 'Old Maid's Winter Apple') dates to 1819 and originates from Sussex. Discovered in a wood in Nottinghamshire and named for the daughter of a local innkeeper, 'Bess Poole' dates from 1824. The fruit has dry, sweet flesh and this is a particularly useful cultivar in frost-prone areas as it flowers later than most apples. Introduced in the 1850s 'Annie Elizabeth' is a cooking apple and possibly a seedling of 'Blenheim Orange', which it resembles in shape, size and its relatively sweet flavour. From Carse of Gowrie in Scotland, 'Bloody Ploughman' dates to the 1880s and is a blood red apple with a mild, sweet flavour.

OPPOSITE *Apples 'Harvey' and 'Cox's Pomona' (suspended, left and right), 'Cox's Pomona' and 'Opalescent' (in bowl), and 'Starkrimson' (left) and 'Annie Elizabeth' (right).* OVERLEAF *Apple 'Cox's Pomona'.*

The common Bramble bringeth foorth slender branches … armed with harde and sharpe prickles … the fruite or berrie is like those of the Mulberie, first red, blacke when it is ripe, in taste betweene sweete and soure, very soft and full of graines.

Gerard, 1597

BLACKBERRY
Rubus fruticosus

The wild bramble is native to Britain and is just one of a number of different species and varieties belonging to the *Rubus* genus that produce blackberries. With a distribution throughout northern Europe and South America, these species typically have perennial roots and biennial canes, and produce an aggregate fruit composed of individual drupelets around a core. However, unlike the raspberry (see p. 72), the core remains attached to the drupelets when picked.

Theophrastus makes mention of the blackberry, as do Pliny and Ovid – the last recalling that blackberries were one of the wild fruits eaten during the Golden Age, along with strawberries, cherries and arbutus berries. Wild-gathered blackberries have been consumed in Britain since Neolithic times, and forensic evidence from the Haraldskær Woman, whose remains were retrieved from a bog in Denmark, reveals she had consumed blackberries before her death in *c.* 490 BC.

In the Dark Ages the blackberry appears as *brer* or *braemel* in both the *Læcboc of Bald* and *Lacnunga* and is the *blaceberian* in Ælfric's *Glossary*. To the Tudor Turner (1548) it was the 'bramble or a blacke bery bush', though no texts mention blackberry cultivation. Gerard (1597) discusses the blackberry, but is the last major author to do so for a couple of centuries. There is no doubt that the blackberry continued to be familiar and popular – as a fresh fruit, a constituent of a blue dye and an ingredient of flavoured ale – but the absence of cultural advice in the gardening literature implies that it was simply gathered from the wild. One piece of folklore states that blackberries should not be picked after Old

Michaelmas Day (11 October, the celebration of the Archangel Michael who defeated Lucifer in the battle for Heaven), for the devil had claimed the fruit, marking the leaves as his by urinating on them. One explanation for this could be the patches of Botrytis mould that may appear on the leaves in autumn.

In 1825 Loudon classified the blackberry among his 'Native, or neglected Fruits, deserving Cultivation', though sparing it a mere paragraph. A year later the (Royal) Horticultural Society was growing 21 types in its Chiswick garden. And it remained in the wilderness until the late 19th century. It was only after the blackberry had been taken to America, hybridized and the new cultivars returned to these shores in the 1860s that it finally sparked some interest. But not much. Even the advent of hybrid berries such as the loganberry (see p. 72), failed to inspire. And the poor blackberry remains undeservedly under appreciated. Thankfully, though, there are a couple of heritage varieties to try. Of American origin and a cultivar of *R. armeniacus* (introduced into Europe in 1835) is 'Himalayan Giant'. Dating to the 1890s, it is very vigorous and produces slightly acidic fruits. Likely a form of the European species *R. laciniatus* that was taken to America, 'Oregon Thornless' (syn. 'Oregon Evergreen Black' and 'Thornless Evergreen') produces an abundance of round berries and also has an ornamental cut-leaf which tints a deep red in autumn.

OPPOSITE *Blackberry 'Oregon Thornless'.*

I shall graff it with a medlar: then it will be the earliest fruit i' the country; for you'll be rotten ere you be half ripe, and that's the right virtue of the medlar.

Shakespeare, *As You Like It*

MEDLAR
Mespilus germanica

Closely related to the genus *Crataegus* (hawthorn) and originating in the Transcaucasia region, the medlar came west via Persia, where it was cultivated by the Assyrians. Theophrastus in the 4th century BC says that it was grown in Greece, from where the medlar must have reached Italy sometime between the mid-2nd century BC, when Cato does not mention it, and the 1st century AD, when Pliny does. The medlar does not seem to have been brought to Britain by the Romans, in which case it was probably an early monastic introduction, arriving before the late 10th century when the fruit is listed by Ælfric and called *æpening* in the *Læcboc of Bald*. The fruit is also named in medieval literary sources including Neckam and the Westminster Abbey Customary of 1270 (see p. 84). Later, royal household accounts reveal that Henry VIII gave medlars as gifts. Turner (1548) somewhat indelicately names it the 'medler tree or an open ars tree'. Take a look at the underneath of the fruit and you will understand what he means.

Gerard mentions four types; a generation later Parkinson lists only three: the greater, the lesser and the Neapolitan. The last is the only medlar named by John Rea in *Pomona* (1665), where he also gives it the name Azarollier. In spite of all the centuries of cultivation, the medlar never became a very popular fruit. In 1697 Worlidge is definite in his opinion that 'the medlar is a fruit of very little use'. Even in the mid-19th century, a time when the popularity of the medlar was at its greatest, M'Intosh states that only five types were in cultivation, of which but three were worth growing: 'Nottingham' (syn. 'Common', 'Narrow-leaved Dutch', 'Small-fruited'), 'Dutch' and 'Monstrous medlar' (syn. 'Neffe Monstrouse'). Of these, the first two remain in cultivation, and are called 'Nottingham' and 'Large Dutch' by Miller in 1731.

The medlar's persistent lack of popularity may in part be because it is an awkward fruit to consume – it cannot be eaten raw, for it is acidic and hard, and to become edible must be 'bletted' (from the French *blettir*, to become overripe or mushy). This entails softening and sweetening by the process of fermentation, either naturally by means of frost or by storing harvested fruits for a few weeks until the flesh begins to decompose slightly. Even when the softened fruit is ready to be eaten out of its brown leathery skin it is an acquired taste. Which begs the question why the medlar was not simply abandoned. One answer could be that the tree, with its big dark green leaves and large white flowers in spring, is very ornamental. In recent years the medlar has enjoyed a minor upsurge in popularity. The cultivar 'Stoneless' is named by Hogg in 1884, while the 'Iranian Medlar' is a recent introduction but has been widely grown in Iran, probably from ancient times, where it is eaten as fresh fruit in late autumn and early winter. It probably originates from wild medlars native to the forests in the Alborz Mountains along the Caspian Sea coast and it is slightly different from European cultivars: a little less vigorous, it has smaller leaves and fruit which ripen a fortnight before European types and which are more elongated in shape and have a relatively closed eye.

OPPOSITE *'Iranian Medlar'.*

NUTS

A nut is a composite of the hard-shelled fruit within which is an indehiscent seed(s) – meaning that on ripening, the fruit (the shell) does not open to release the seed(s). Because many nuts have a high oil and calorie content they have been an important part of the human diet for 780,000 years: archaeological sites dating to the Pleistocene period have yielded tools made by prehistoric humans to crack open nuts.

ALMOND
Prunus dulcis

The almond is closely related to the apricot, cherry, peach, plum and nectarine. But what we consume is reversed. Rather than eating the skin and the flesh, in the case of the almond what we eat is the seed, discarding everything else. The almond is native to the Middle East as far east as the Indus, and domestication took place in the Near East during the Early Bronze Age (*c.* 3000–2000 BC). No doubt the process resulted in untimely death for some since the seed of wild almonds contains a substance called amygdalin, which when chewed is converted into hydrogen cyanide. This characteristic has been bred out in the edible sweet almond but is still present in the bitter almond (*P. dulcis* var. *amara*), the extract of which was once used medicinally.

Known to the Minoans of Bronze Age Crete, the almond also makes several appearances in the Old Testament. In Genesis it is described as 'among the best of fruits' (43:11). In ancient Phrygia its early blooming and heralding of spring may have been a reason for the almond's esteemed position as Father of All Things. Almonds were found in Tutankhamun's tomb (*c.* 1323 BC) and were consumed by the ancient Greeks, who also extracted oil from the seeds. The almond may have travelled north from Africa via Crete or west from Persia and was in cultivation on mainland Greece by *c.* 500 BC. It was from Greece that the Romans acquired what they called 'the Greek nut'; the word 'almond' derives from the Greek *amygdale* through the Latin *amandola* and the Old French *almande*. Pliny and Columella both discuss the almond, and excepting the pine nut it is the most frequently used nut in the recipes of Apicius.

Archaeological evidence reveals that the Romans consumed almonds in Britain and it is thought that the tree was in cultivation here. If not then, it was soon introduced by religious houses, for the almond is named by Ælfric, Neckam and Chaucer. In 1548 Turner says that the 'almon' was grown in 'fieldes' in Italy and 'high Germany' but only in gardens in England. It was familiar to Gerard and Parkinson, the latter offering a range of medicinal uses for almond oil. Mawe in his *The British Fruit Garden* (1779) describes five types and praises it highly, saying the almond is 'eminent both as a fruit tree, and for ornamenting the shrubbery, &c. early in spring' and that it deserves a place in 'almost every garden'. Yet Mawe's enthusiasm does not appear to have been shared by all gardeners: in 1831 John Lindley states that because the 'description of fruit being little known in Great Britain' he will offer a list 'of the [eight] principal varieties cultivated in France' – only one of which, 'Princess', remains in cultivation. Another heritage almond is the American cultivar 'Texas Mission', which was discovered as a chance seedling in 1891.

OPPOSITE *Almonds.*

The shell is smooth and woodie; the kernell within consisteth of a white, hard, and sound pulpe ... oftentimes red, most commonly white; this kernell is sweete and pleasant to the taste.

Gerard, 1597

NUTS

COB NUT & FILBERT

Corylus avellana & *C. maxima*

The name hazelnut applies to nuts of any species of the genus *Corylus*. Thus the nut of *Corylus avellana* is both a hazelnut and more specifically the cob nut. Cob nuts are roughly spherical to oval, with an outer fibrous husk surrounding a smooth shell. Native to western Asia and Europe including Britain, cob nuts collected from the wild have long been part of the human diet. For example, on the Inner Hebridean island of Colonsay archaeologists discovered evidence of large-scale nut processing radiocarbon-dated to *c.* 7000 BC. The filbert (*C. maxima*), on the other hand, is native to southwestern Asia and southeastern Europe, from Turkey to the Balkans, and the nut itself is elongated, being about twice as long as it is round. The etymology of 'filbert' is Norman French. The feast day of St Philibert of Jumièges (*c.* 608–84) is 22 August, about the same date that the nuts are ready for harvest.

Theophrastus is the first to write about the cultivated hazelnut as well as one he says has an oblong nut, which is probably the filbert. However, Pliny says the filbert came to Italy from Pontus (a region on the southern coast of the Black Sea in northeastern Turkey). In Britain the hazelnut appears in early texts, but because of its widespread natural occurrence the shrubby tree does not seem to have been taken into garden cultivation until the 16th century. When filberts appeared is obscure, but they were not a Roman import and since they appear alongside hazelnuts in the medieval and Tudor literature, a monastic introduction in the Dark Ages seems likely. In 1375 'filberdis' were harvested at Kingston in Dorset and in 1573 Tusser recommends that 'red and white filbeardes' be grown in the garden – both cultivars remain in cultivation. Gerard (1597) illustrates the common cob nut together with the 'Filberd', the 'Filberd Nut

of Constantinople' (*C. colurna*) and also describes the 'Turky nut', which produces nuts of a smaller size than the native hazelnut. Mawe (1779) adds to the classificatory confusion by grouping together filberts and cob nuts as selected varieties of the native 'common wood nut'. He adds that the filbert is the most widely cultivated nut in gardens and orchards, but also advocated planting the 'very large' cob nut.

It appears therefore that by the turn of the 19th century a range of *Corylus* species was cultivated in gardens and orchards, known by a variety of names. By 1884 there was no improvement in the clarity of classification, for Hogg divided nuts into four groups: Filberts, Spanish, Cobs and Hazel nuts. The Spanish nut he classified as *C. algeriensis*. He proceeded to describe 32 types of nut, of which 11 remain in cultivation. Raised by Richard Webb of Calcot near Reading are 'Cannon Ball' and 'Daviana' ('named as a compliment to Sir Humphrey Davy'). Introduced in 1816, with a thin shell and originating from Ipswich, 'Cosford' is described as 'An excellent nut, and the tree is a great bearer'. 'Liegel's Zellernuss' was raised by 'Dr Liegel, of Braunau, a distinguished pomologist'. One of the finest new introductions is the 'Kentish Cob', listed by Hogg as 'Lambert's Filbert'. It is believed that the cultivar was named for or by Mr Aylmer Bourke Lambert of Boynton in Wiltshire, who brought it to the attention of the (Royal) Horticultural Society in 1812. The others are 'Frizzled Filbert' (mentioned by Loudon in 1825), 'Pearson's Prolific', 'Burchardt's Zellernuss', 'The Shah' and the above mentioned white and red filberts.

OPPOSITE *Cob nuts.*

The chestnut has its armour of defence in a shell bristling with prickles like the hedge-hog … Chestnuts are the most pleasant eating when roasted: they are sometimes ground also, and are eaten by women when fasting for religious scruples.

Pliny, 1st century AD

NUTS

SWEET CHESTNUT

Castanea sativa

Native to Asia Minor and southeastern Europe, the fruit of the sweet chestnut or Marron is contained within a spiny, prickly cupule (technically a specially adapted part of the pseudocarp that occurs in some members of the beech family Fagaceae), which protects the developing fruit and splits at maturity to release the nuts. Domestication of the sweet chestnut is believed to have taken place in the Balkans region in the middle of the 2nd millennium BC and the nut has proven its worth in many different culinary applications. Particularly in areas where wheat or grains do not grow readily, it is ground to make a flour, while in Corsica it is used to brew a form of beer. One possible suggestion for the etymology of its genus name is that the tree came from Kastania, a town in Thessaly in northeastern Greece, but of course it may be the other way around – the town took its name from the trees growing there.

Certainly the Greek army was thankful for its supply of chestnuts, which reputedly saved the soldiers from starvation during a retreat from Asia Minor in 401–399 BC. It may have been this near-disaster that inspired Alexander the Great, according to legend, to plant chestnut trees along the routes of his campaigns, a policy later adopted by the Romans, who spread the tree into northern Europe and to Britain, where it remained in cultivation. Pliny has a chapter on 18 varieties of chestnut and Apicius included a recipe for chestnuts with lentils.

The chestnut tree is very long lived and the 'Great Chestnut of Tortworth' (a hamlet in Gloucestershire) is shown on boundary records from the time of King John, who reigned 1199–1216. In 1720 the trunk measured in excess of 15 m (50 ft) at 1.5 m (5 ft) above the ground. It is the French, however, who have perhaps cultivated, developed and eaten the sweet chestnut most – especially in the crystallized or candied form of marrons glacés.

OPPOSITE *Sweet chestnuts.*

The common walnut being raised from seeds there are a great number
of varieties among those grown in this country, varying in size,
flavour, thickness of the shell, and fertility. To secure a variety of a
certain character, it must be perpetuated by grafting.

Hogg, 1884

NUTS

WALNUT
Juglans regia

Botanically the walnut is a drupe fruit and thus similar to the almond (see p. 136), while technically it is the edible seed of any member of the genus *Juglans*. But specifically we eat the seed of the Persian, English or Common walnut. Native to a zone from the Balkans east to the Himalaya and southwest to China, the walnut is a particular feature of Kyrgyzstan, where at an altitude of between 1,000 and 2,000 m (3,300 to 6,600 ft) there are forests consisting almost exclusively of walnut trees. The tree was probably brought into domestication *c.* 1500 BC. In the 4th century BC Alexander the Great introduced into Greece what Theophrastus calls the Persian nut, and it was cultivated by the Greeks and Romans. According to Pliny both called it *nux Gallica*, the Gallic nut – perhaps reflecting acquisition of the tree from the Gaulish region of Galatia in Anatolia – and honoured it with the name *iovis glandem* or nut of Jove (Jupiter), from which comes *Juglans*.

The introduction of the walnut into Britain – our word derives from the Old English *walhhnutu*, meaning foreign nut – was by the Romans, and although named by Ælfric (*c.* 995), it is absent from other medieval sources. This perhaps suggests that the tree fell out of cultivation; if so it had been reintroduced by the mid-13th century since an entry in the accounts of the Earl of Lincoln's garden in Holborn for 1295–96 reveals a substantial income of £9 for pears, apples and 'great nuts' or walnuts. It would appear from this that the walnut was a luxury item, a status emphasized again in the Durham Account Rolls for 1369 when 2,000 'Walsnotes' cost 2s 6d.

As with so many fruits a boom in walnut cultivation began in the 16th century. In 1548 Turner noted that the walnut was so well known that he did not need to describe it. Twelve years later Holinshed's *Chronicles* reported that the types of walnut introduced in the previous 40 years were far superior to those formerly in cultivation; and by 1597 Gerard confirmed that the walnut was cultivated in both orchards and gardens. By 1629 Parkinson could also include a new arrival, *Juglans nigra*, the Virginian black walnut from North America. Yet in spite of the enthusiasm with which the walnut was planted, its success was hampered by the changing climate. The Little Ice Age began in 1550 and successive years' harvests were hit by late frosts, necessitating the import of nuts from Italy. Walnut wood remained in demand for furniture until the arrival of mahogany in the late 18th century.

Because of the difficulties of asexually propagating (cloning) walnuts by grafting and from cuttings, trees were primarily raised from seed – in 1929 it was estimated that 99 per cent of walnuts growing in the United Kingdom were seed grown. Little attempt has therefore ever been made to breed new cultivars. New introductions did come from abroad – though not many. In the 5th edition of the compendious *The Fruit Manual* (1884), Hogg lists only seven, several with French names, including 'À Coque Tendre' or 'Thin Shelled', and 'Tardif' or 'Saint Jean', as well as 'Highflyer' and 'Yorkshire'.

OPPOSITE *Walnuts.*

PEAR

Pyrus communis subsp. *communis*

The genus *Pyrus* contains about 20 species and is thought to have arisen in the Tian Shan mountains of Central Asia. For centuries before it was domesticated, the archaeological record reveals that across Europe this fruit was gathered from the wild. The cultivated pear is believed to be derived from one or two wild subspecies which are widely distributed throughout Europe (*P. communis* subsp. *pyraster* and *P. communis* subsp. *caucasica*), and the name 'pear' probably derives from the Common West Germanic *pera*.

> Some peares are sweete, divers fat and unctuous, others sower, and most are harsh, especially the wilde Peares, and some consist of divers mixtures of tastes, and some having no taste at all.
>
> Gerard, 1597

The first account of pear cultivation is by Homer, who tells us in *The Odyssey* that the trees grew in the orchard of Alcinous, along with apples (see p. 12). The Greeks and Romans both eagerly grew domesticated pears: Cato and Varro discuss their cultivation and Pliny describes a wide range of types, many named after the region they originated. He confidently states that 'All the world are extremely partial to the Crustumium' and that the 'Falernian' pears are used to make wine. He later adds the information that the pear was not eaten raw because it was harmful to health, but was 'wholesome' if cooked. Apicius obligingly provides a recipe.

The pear is another in the long line of Roman fruit introductions into Britain. The name *peran* appears in the *Læcboc of Bald* in the 10th century, and in 1086 Domesday Book records pear trees used as boundary markers, so presumably they must have been already well-established and recognizable features. The 13th century saw many new gardens laid out, and pears played a role both in the ornamental garden (herber) and orchard. And the cultivars grown were French (La Rochelle was especially famed for its pears) or German. Royal accounts reveal that in 1223 Henry III purchased in France 'S. Rule' (also 'Rewel' and 'St Regolo'); the king clearly liked pears, because in 1252 he also bought 'Janettar', 'Sorelles' and 'Cailloels' ('Cailhou'). A decade later he ordered six more 'Cailhou' for planting in his Westminster garden. Henry's son, Edward I, also planted 'Cailhou' and 'Rewel' at Westminster between 1276 and 1292. The pears harvested then were still little different from the ones described by Pliny – the fruits were hard, grainy or gritty, and not eaten fresh off the tree; they were instead cooked, or if not tasty turned into perry (pear cider). The former is certainly true of the most famous early English cultivar that is still available. According to Hogg (1884) 'Warden' (or 'Wardon') was raised by the Cistercian monks of Wardon Abbey in Bedfordshire sometime before 1388. With its firm-textured flesh, this cultivar was renowned for making excellent pies and was served in syrup at Henry IV's wedding feast. As the clown says in Shakespeare's *The Winter's Tale*: 'I must have saffron to colour the Warden pies'.

From a high point in the 14th century, pears, like other orchard fruit, declined in the 15th only to be revived in the 16th century with another injection of different kinds from abroad. The result was a flush of new English cultivars, but as Gerard (1597) pointed out, not all were worth growing. While Pliny mentioned 36 types, Parkinson (1629) restricted himself to 66, including some that dated back to the 13th century, but most were new, including the 'Spanish pear', which had been introduced

OPPOSITE *Pears 'Chaumontel' (left), 'Black Worcester' (centre) and 'Bishop's Thumb' (right).*

> The most excellent sorts of Peares, serve … to make an after-course for their masters table, where the goodnesse of his Orchard is tryed. … They are eaten familiarly of all sorts of people, of some for delight, and of others for nourishment, being baked, stewed, or scalded.
>
> Parkinson, 1629

by his friend John Tradescant in 1611. From Parkinson's list a couple remain in cultivation, for instance 'Gergonell' is now 'Jargonelle', while 'Windsor' has kept its name.

Sir Thomas Hanmer penned his *Garden Book* in 1659, but the manuscript was subsequently lost for nearly three centuries before at last being published in 1933. In this delightful book Hanmer names the French cultivar 'Winter Bon Chrétien'. Considered by the French author and pear authority Jean-Baptiste de la Quintinye (1624–88) as the best of all pears, it remains in cultivation as 'Bon-Chrétien d'Hiver'. Today regarded as a superior dessert pear, it was originally a cooker. Both de la Quintinye and Hogg thought this was the Roman pear 'Crustumium', brought to France in 1495 when Charles VIII returned from his conquest of the Kingdom of Naples. Parkinson says that the best 'Winter Bon Chrétien' is 'the kinde that groweth at Syon', and that the 'Bon Chretien of Syon' is also the 'ten pound peare, or the hundred pound peare', so-called because the grafts cost Henry Percy, the 9th or 'Wizard' Earl of Northumberland (1564–1632), 'so much the fetching by the messengers expences, when he brought nothing else'.

The French favourite 'Beurré du Roy' was first described in 1608 and is a very early buttery or 'melting fleshed' pear. This cultivar marks the beginning of the evolution of the pear as a fruit to be eaten uncooked, and was very influential in the subsequent development of the dessert pear. 'Beurré du Roy' remains available as 'Beurré Brown'.

An important British pear from the 18th century is 'Williams' Bon Chrétien' (which became known in the US as the Bartlett pear), raised by a schoolmaster from Aldermaston in Berkshire named Stair and distributed from 1770 by the nurseryman Williams of Turnham Green in London. But this it seems was the exception to the rule, for as late as 1855 M'Intosh in *The Book of the Garden* states that although 'our present nursery catalogues enumerate nearly 400 … until within the last thirty

or forty years we had few pears possessing the most moderate qualities'. As with most fruits, the 19th century saw both pear cultivar numbers and fruit quality rise rapidly, with the French continuing to lead the way. The century's most important new cultivar, 'Doyenné du Comice' (1849), was brought to England in 1859 by Sir Thomas Dyke Acland, probably to his Devon property on what is now the Holnicote Estate. With its pale yellow, extremely melting and juicy flesh, and a delicate, delicious flavour 'Comice' remains a favourite to this day.

Thankfully today's gardener has a good choice of heritage pear varieties to choose from. In addition to those already named, 'Chaumontel' is a French cultivar dating from *c.* 1660 with very sweet, white, melting flesh and a smooth texture. Also from France and the 17th century is 'Bellisime d'Hiver', an excellent cooking pear with white, tender flesh. From the same century but from northern Saxony in Germany is 'Forelle', which translates as 'trout'. The fruit are small, the flesh fairly firm and the texture crisp. From Normandy, 'Louise Bonne of Jersey' dates to 1788. A reasonable assumption would be that introduction to Britain was via the Channel Island of Jersey. As for Louise, she presumably was someone known to the breeder, a M. Longueval of Avranches, as he originally called the pear simply 'Louise'. It is a large pear with pink-tinged, juicy flesh of a smooth texture. Of 'Swan's Egg', Lindley (1831) says the following: 'its great certainty in bearing, and the excellence of its fruit, render it an universal favourite'. 'Black Worcester' is an ancient pear that appears on that city's crest. And introduced to Britain in 1835 by Mr Stoeffels of Mechlin, Belgium, 'Double de Guerre' has firm yellow and slightly acid flesh and is a good cooking pear.

OPPOSITE: ABOVE *Pear 'Frangipane'*; BELOW LEFT *pear 'Levard'*; BELOW RIGHT *pear 'Black Worcester'*. OVERLEAF *Pears 'Bishop's Thumb' (left)*, *'Double de Guerre' (centre) and 'Louise Bonne of Jersey' (right)*.

PLUM

The plum is a stone or drupe fruit (see p. 41), and the domesticated plum is believed to be a hybrid of the sloe or blackthorn (P. spinosa*), native to Britain, and a variety of cherry plum (P.* cerasifera *var.* divaricata*), and to have arisen in the Caucasus region. Today domesticated plums are divided into four variants: common plums; damsons and bullaces; round plums including gages; and the mirabelle.*

COMMON PLUM
Prunus domestica

The plum seems not to have been well known to the Greeks – Theophrastus makes but a passing mention of it – and the first to offer advice on plum cultivation in Italy are Columella and Pliny in the 1st century AD. From the fact that the plum was familiar to Pliny, who expresses surprise that Cato made no mention of it two centuries earlier, it seems that the plum, like the medlar (p. 135), was introduced into Italy between the mid-2nd century BC and the mid-1st century AD. After a late start, however, the Romans made quick advances in plum culture and Pliny was able to describe 'a vast crowd' of 12 types, including the 'Armenian' and the damson, 'so-called from Damascus in Syria'.

In Britain, Bronze and Iron Age sites have yielded evidence of consumption of the native blackthorn, but it was the Romans who brought the domesticated plum and the cherry plum (*P. cerasifera*), which nowadays is primarily grown as an ornamental. Called the plum as early as its entry in the *Læcboc of Bald*, the fruit appears in all the major English and European texts from *Capitulare de Villis* in the late 8th century onwards. The plum is also one of the staples set down in the Westminster Abbey Customary of 1270 (se p. 84), and another indication of its popularity and importance is the mention of 'ploumes' by Chaucer in *The Romaunt of the Rose* (1372).

Again as with many orchard fruits, after a decline in 15th century an impetus for the revival of the plum came with Henry VIII's policy to bring new life to English orchards in the 16th century through the introduction of cultivars from abroad. Yet in Tudor times, as in the centuries before, the plum was still cultivated in order to produce a dried fruit consumed the year round, rather than eaten fresh. The impact of prunes on the Tudor diet was recorded by Peter Treveris in his *Grete Herball* (1526): 'Plomes; They have vertue to smothe and polyshe y bowelles'.

By 1597 Gerard was not only growing many different types of plum, but his writings also confirm that most of the new types were introductions rather than English-bred. Parkinson (1629) says that his 'very good friend' John Tradescant is an expert on plums, and through his labours

OPPOSITE *Plum 'Bountiful'.*

There ar a greate sorte of diverse kyndes of plumbes, one with a diverse color, an other black an other whytishe. There ar other that they call barley plumbes of the folowyng of that corn. … These kindes of gardin plumbes (if a man may trust Pliny) were not knowe in Italie in Catoes tyme.

Turner, 1562

abroad gathering together new types had developed a large and rare collection at Hatfield House (see p. 19). Parkinson provides descriptions of 62 types, including 'The Margate plum the worst of an hundred', while the 'white diapred plum of Malta, scarce knowne to any in our Land but John Tradescante, is a very good plum'. Some remain in cultivation, for instance the Damson, Mirobalane (probably the Mirabelle; see p. 162), and 'Amber Primordian', which is considered to be 'Catalonia' and is one of the first cultivars to ripen.

By the start of the 18th century the gardener had somewhere in the region of 70 cultivars to choose from, many of which dated to the earlier part of the previous century. By the end of the 18th century the same cultivars were on offer, revealing that little had occurred in the way of British plum breeding for two centuries. One notable exception, and still in cultivation, is 'Coe's Golden Drop', which was raised by Jervaise Coe, a market gardener living in Suffolk, and introduced in 1800. This new arrival was a sign of things to come. The (Royal) Horticultural Society encouraged plum breeding and for once it was not Thomas Andrew Knight (see p. 42), who had so much success with cherries, who was the hero. His attempts came to little, and the 19th century's 'Plum King' was Thomas Rivers of Rivers Nursery in Hertfordshire (see p. 41), who introduced over 20 new cultivars including 'Early Prolific' (syn. 'River's Early Prolific'), 'Early Rivers' (raised 1820, introduced 1834), 'Damson Early Rivers' (1871), 'Early Transparent Gage' (1873; see p. 159) and 'Czar' (1874), all of which remain in cultivation. Rivers' successors continued

his work and 'President' is a dual-purpose plum (a cooker and an eater) introduced in 1901 and notable for its large, later ripening fruit, which have a lovely deep purple skin and sharp and sweet yellow flesh.

But today's favourite plum is another of those accidental discoveries. Found growing in a garden in Alderton in Sussex and sold to Denyer, a nurseryman at Brixton in London, 'Victoria' was introduced in 1840. Popular because it produces huge quantities of medium-sized fruits which have a lovely reddy-purple colour, yellow flesh and a sweet/tart taste, it does have two drawbacks – brittle wood and susceptibility to disease. Of other surviving heritage varieties, 'Bountiful', raised in 1900 by the famous Bedford nursery Laxton Bros, Ltd and introduced in 1926, has firm but not very juicy fruits with a flavour that is slightly sweet. Of more recent vintage, 'Dundale' has golden yellow, egg-shaped plums which have firm flesh and little juice (or flavour). It originated in Kent in 1920 and is said to be the original 'Warwickshire Drooper'. Raised in Leicester by T. G. Smith, 'Golden Monarch' has greenish skin and firm, very juicy, moderately sweet flesh. Plum 'George Calver' is said to have arisen as a chance seedling in a garden in Devon in 1966. And 'Vision', although raised in 1937 at the Horticultural Research Institute of Ontario, Vineland Station, was not introduced until 1967. It is a beautiful fruit with dark purple skin and greeny-yellow sweet and juicy flesh.

OPPOSITE: ABOVE *Plum 'Bountiful'*; BELOW LEFT *plum 'Golden Monarch'*; BELOW RIGHT *plum 'George Calver'*. OVERLEAF *Plum 'President'*.

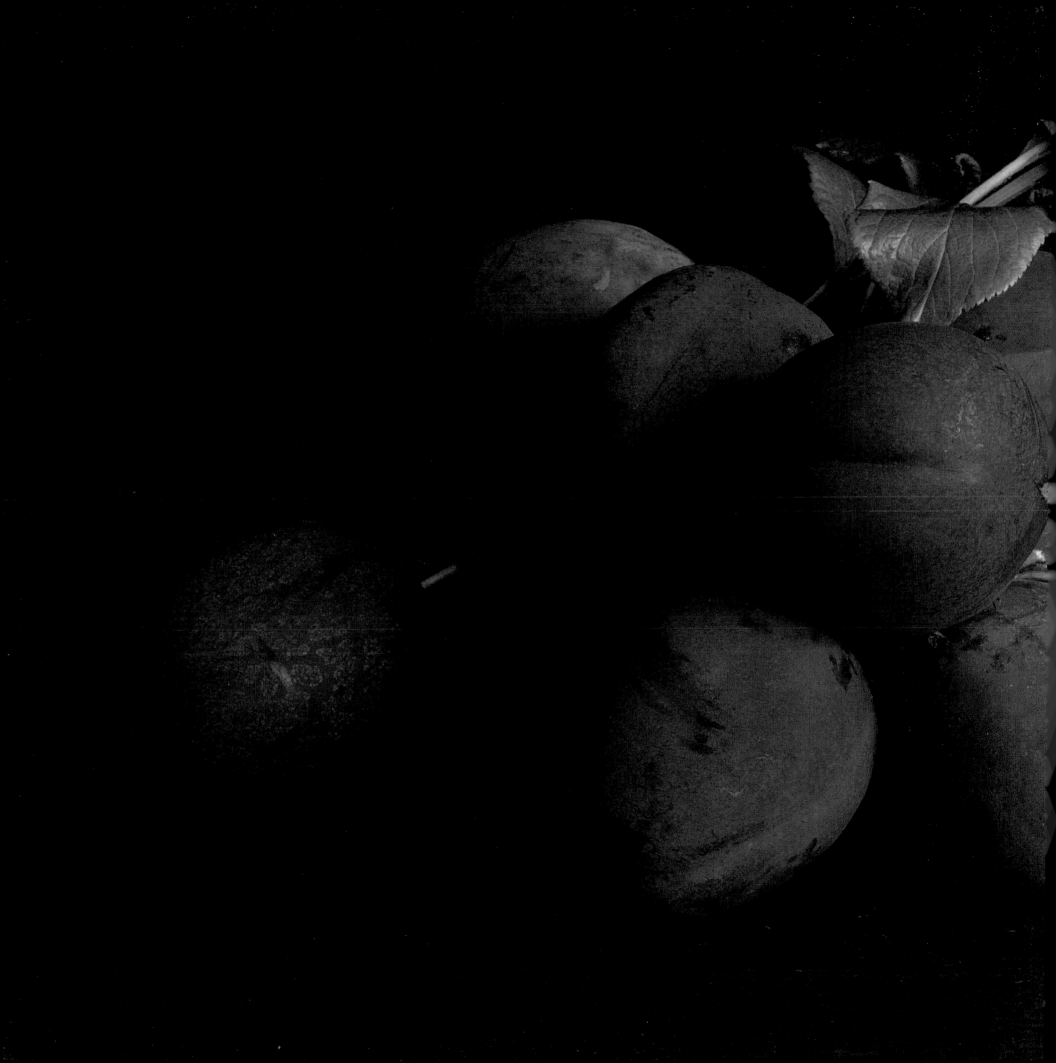

La grosse Reine Claude, i.e. the large Queen Claudia, by some the Dauphiny. … This is one of the best plums in England; it is of a middle size, round, and of a yellowish green colour on the outside; the flesh is firm, of a deep green colour, and parts from the stone; the juice has an exceeding rich flavour, and it is a great bearer.

Miller, 1768

PLUM

GAGE
Prunus domestica

Gages are identified by their small, oval-shaped fruits, ranging in colour from green to yellow, which possess smooth-textured and often melting flesh. The cultivar 'Old Greengage' was developed in Moissac in France from an original form that came to that country from Armenia, via Greece and Italy. In France it is called 'Reine Claude', in honour of Claude, Duchess of Brittany, the queen consort of King François I in the early 16th century. This plum was universally admired by authors and acquired its English name on its arrival from France, though by accident. In 1831 Lindley, agreeing with Miller (1768), exclaimed 'This is, without exception, the best Plum in England', and recounted how it had been procured in the previous century (1724 is given as a date) from 'the Monks of the Chartreuse at Paris'. However, the label had been lost in transit and so the gardener simply called it Green Gage for his employer, Sir William Gage of Sussex.

Raised by W. H. Divers of Hook in Surrey, 'Wierton Gage' was introduced in 1934. A little older is 'Merton Gage', which was bred in 1923 at the John Innes Horticultural Institute in the London Borough of Merton by M. B. Crane and named *c.* 1952. The fruits have a very attractive red-blushed yellow skin and a moderately juicy, sweet and rich-flavoured flesh. Another 20th-century introduction is 'Apricot Gage', originally found in the Honeybourne district of Worcestershire. The russet-pink skin contrasts beautifully with the apricot-coloured, slightly juicy and sweet flesh. Transparent gages, such as 'Early Transparent Gage' (see p. 153) have thin, almost translucent skin and flesh.

OPPOSITE: ABOVE *Plum 'Apricot Gage'*; BELOW LEFT *plum 'Merton Gage'*; BELOW RIGHT *plum 'Wierton Gage'*. OVERLEAF *Plum 'Apricot Gage'*.

The White Mirable … is a small Amber-colour'd Plumb, and a
great bearer; its Pulp comes from the Stone, and is vastly rich,
with a fine delicious sugar'd Juice. The Fruits are very richly
sugar'd, even when produc'd on Standards, or Dwarfs,
but much finer against an East or South-East Wall.

Langley, 1729

PLUM

MIRABELLE

Prunus insititia

Sweet and full of flavour, the mirabelle plum has a characteristically small, oval shape, with smooth-textured flesh. Its skin is often a yellow colour, which becomes attractively freckled. The mirabelle is an ornamental small tree when in bloom and is believed to have originated in Asia Minor. It has been a speciality of the Lorraine region of northeast France ever since the arrival of 'Mirabelle de Nancy' in the 15th century, followed in 1675 by 'Mirabelle de Metz', both named after towns in the area. It is still much celebrated there – Metz holds an annual mirabelle festival every summer, and since 1996 the local mirabelle has been recognized and protected as a regional product by the European Union.

In his chapter on 'Plumbs' in *Pomona: or, the Fruit-Garden Illustrated* (1729), Batty Langley includes among his list of the 'very great Variety' of this fruit the 'White Mirable'. Miller (1768) says 'La Mirabelle' is a 'small round fruit, of a greenish yellow on the outside' and 'is excellent for sweetmeats'. This plum is indeed particularly favoured for jams and pies, most notably the 'tarte aux Mirabelles', but is also delicious eaten raw when ripe. In addition, its juice can be made into a plum wine or distilled into brandy and eau de vie.

OPPOSITE *Mirabelle plums.*

QUINCE
Cydonia oblonga

Native to east Transcaucasia, wild quinces still grow in great numbers in the forests of Azerbaijan. But it seems it was in Mesopotamia that this pome fruit (see p. 126) was first domesticated and cultivated. It is an ancient fruit – the Greeks grew it, so did the Romans. Pliny observed that the tree grew abundantly on Crete, hence its genus name is derived from the town of Cydonia, now Chania, on the northwest coast of the island. In Greek mythology, Ladon, the serpent-dragon in the Garden of the Hesperides, may have been guarding a quince tree with its golden yellow fruit rather than an apple, and so it may have been a quince that Paris awarded Aphrodite, having been bribed with the prize of Helen (see p. 126). To the Romans the quince was a symbol of love, happiness and fruitfulness. Plutarch in his *Roman Questions*, quoting Solon, the early 6th-century BC Athenian lawmaker, recounts the anecdote that 'in order that the first greeting may not be disagreeable nor unpleasant' a Greek bride would nibble a quince to perfume her kiss before entering the bridal chamber.

The quince was on Charlemagne's list, the *Capitulare de Villis,* showing its presence in northern Europe by this date. The first English source to mention it is Alexander Neckam in the late 13th century, which suggests that the quince was a monastic or Norman introduction. Certainly it does not appear in the Romano-British archaeological record. Royal accounts for 1277–78 reveal that William le Gardener supplied three quinces and two peach trees for 3s to be planted in Edward I's new herber at the Tower of London. In such small numbers and at a relatively high price (in comparison cherry trees only cost 1s 6d per hundred), it seems that quinces (and peaches) were both uncommon and planted primarily as ornamentals. The relative rarity of the quince as a cultivated plant in England (or the premium price of imported fruit) is demonstrated in 1292, when Edward's wife, Eleanor of Castile, perhaps in order make membrillo – quince paste or cheese – to remind her of her homeland, purchased quince fruit at 4s per hundred, when ordinary apples cost a mere 3d per hundred.

In the mid-16th and 17th centuries Tusser, Gerard and Parkinson were all in turn enthusiastic about the quince, Gerard describing it as the base of 'excellent, dainty and wholesome confections … such as jellies'. Parkinson was the first to describe different named types, including the pear-shaped 'Portingall', which remains in cultivation as 'Portugal'.

In terms of the quince's worth as a fruit, Mawe (1779) puts it succinctly: 'Quinces are valued principally only as a culinary fruit for stewing, baking, making marmalade, and to enrich the flavour of Apple-pies, tarts, &c as being of a very heightened fragrance when fully ripe, but generally too hard and astringent to eat raw'. And yet, with the exception of the widespread practice of using quince rootstock on which to graft pear trees, the quince has been left out in the cold almost ever since it arrived in Britain. An enthusiastic minority champion this wonderful fruit, but few gardeners grow it. The inclusive Loudon (1825) and M'Intosh (1855) can barely fill a couple of paragraphs each, and the normally exhaustive Hogg's list of fruits cultivated (1884), which runs to 759 pages, includes the same three types Mawe listed a century earlier: apple-shaped, pear-shaped and Portugal quince. Of the three Hogg considers 'Portugal' superior, 'the fruit being much milder in flavour, and better adapted for marmalade and stewing'. So here I wave my quince flag and encourage you to try one. Not only is the fruit beautiful, delicious and intoxicatingly perfumed, but the tree is also highly ornamental when in blossom. 'Meech's Prolific' is an American cultivar raised by the Reverend William Witler Meech of Connecticut before 1850. 'Vranja' is of Serbian origin and came to Britain during the inter-war years, and 'Sobu' produces very large pear-shaped quinces.

OPPOSITE: ABOVE *Quinces 'Meech's Prolific' (left), 'Sobu' (at the back), 'Portugal' (front left) and 'Vranja';* BELOW LEFT *quince 'Portugal';* BELOW RIGHT *quince 'Vranja'.*

Sellery … was formerly a stranger with us (nor very long since in Italy).
… The tender leaves of the Blancht Stalk do well in our Sallet,
as likewise the slices of the whiten'd Stems, which being crimp and
short, first peel'd and slit long wise, are eaten with Oyl, Vinegar, Salt,
and Peper; and for its high and grateful taste, is ever plac'd in
the middle of the Grand Sallet, at our Great Mens Tables.

Evelyn, 1699

AUTUMN VEGETABLES

CELERY & CELERIAC

Apium graveolens var. *dulce* & *A. graveolens* var. *rapaceum*

The species *Apium graveolens* is a relative of the carrot and native to Asia, North Africa and Europe, including Britain, where it was called 'smallage' by early English writers. In domesticated forms it is the crisp petiole (leaf stalk) that is consumed in the case of celery and the swollen basal stem base in the case of celeriac. Both types have been selected and bred to improve the particular desired characteristic.

In use by 1664 the word 'celery' derives from the French *céleri*, in turn from Italian *seleri* and the ancient Greek *selinon* meaning 'parsley', a word that first appears in Linear B tablets from Mycenaean Greece. Celery leaves and flower heads were woven into garlands in the tomb of Tutankhamun (*c.* 1323 BC), but whether this was a wild or domesticated form is unclear. Homer in *The Odyssey* tells us of meadows of violet and wild celery surrounding Calypso's cave on the island of Ogygia. Celery leaves were used in Classical Greece to make wreaths – both for the dead and also for the victors at the Isthmian and Nemean games.

The cultivated form of celery may have come to Britain with the Romans, but later evidence suggests that if it did, it fell from cultivation. Celery appears in all the major medieval and Tudor texts, although there seems to be little to indicate a domesticated form. John Evelyn's enthusiastic description in *Acetaria* (1699) would suggest that garden celery was introduced late, sometime towards the end of the 17th century. Celery was also boiled and consumed as a vegetable throughout the 18th century, although according to James Wheeler's *The Botanist's and Gardener's Dictionary* (1758) it was 'seldom cultivated in gardens'. Yet Mawe offers cultural advice in 1782, expounding the benefits of 'earthing up' in order to blanch the stems. By the mid-19th century M'Intosh also provides advice on 'wintering' the crop – storing it *in situ* and erecting a shelter over the trenches of plants.

A number of heritage varieties are available, including two from the 18th century: 'Solid White' (syn. 'Celeri Turc') was in cultivation by 1787 and has 'stalks broad, thick, crisp & tender', the stems blanching to about 30 cm (1 ft) in length, while dating prior to 1793 is 'Cutting' (syn. 'Soup'), which is basically wild celery. A favourite American cultivar, 'Green Utah' is self-blanching and produces tall, crisp, bright green stems.

Celeriac has been selected for its large and bulbous hypocotyl, the area of stem below the cotyledons or seed leaves and above the radicle or root. The absence of what can categorically be identified as celeriac from the literature before Bauhin's *Historia plantarum universalis* (1651) suggests this selection also occurred in the 17th century, making celeriac another late addition to the kitchen garden. Stephen Switzer in 1728 states that he had never seen it, and that a gentleman who had long been an importer of curious seeds furnished him with a supply from Alexandria. Celeriac remained little known or appreciated in Britain. As late as 1855 M'Intosh offers only passing mention. And it remains a minority interest vegetable, perhaps because it is such a fiddle to clean and prepare; some describe it as the octopus vegetable on account of its root mass. The cultivar 'Prinz' produces a large, round 'root' which has crisp white flesh, and 'Giant Prague' (by 1871) is another recommended heritage variety of which it was said that 'gradually more gardeners are becoming acquainted with this splendid vegetable, which is much easier to grow than Celery'.

OPPOSITE *Celeriac 'Prinz' and celery 'Green Utah'.*

There is likewise another sort hereof … the which has leaves very great and red of colour, as is all the rest of the plant … the middle ribbe of which leaves are for the most part verie broad and thicke, like the middle part of the Cabbage leafe, which is equall in goodnesse with the leaves of Cabbage being boiled.

Gerard, 1597

CHARD

Beta vulgaris subsp. *cicla*

Known by a variety of names including leaf beet, Swiss chard, silverbeet, spinach beet and perpetual spinach, chard is cultivated for its leaves, with their enlarged midribs and stems. In recent years it has also become popular to grow the brightly coloured cultivars as ornamentals. Closely related to the beetroot, chard is believed to be descended from the wild sea beet (*Beta vulgaris* subsp. *maritima*), which is native to Britain, and to be of Mediterranean, probably Sicilian, origin.

Chard was familiar to the Greeks, who had a colony on Sicily, and the various different coloured forms were noted by several authors: the red by Aristotle (*c.* 350 BC) and the white and dark green by Theophrastus and Dioscorides. It was also a popular vegetable for discussion by Roman authors – Apicius, Columella, Palladius and Pliny all write about it. Although sea beet seed is found in the archaeological record of Roman Britain, it is not possible to distinguish between the seed of native and domesticated forms, and so it is not certain that the Romans introduced the latter. However, given the increased occurrence within the archaeological record over time and the fact that chard was a popular Roman vegetable it would appear likely.

Yet if so, chard seems to have disappeared from the medieval garden (although it may be Albertus Magnus's *acelga*), for it is not mentioned in any of the texts. It re-emerges in the literature of the 17th and 18th centuries and four types are described. Named 'Swiss or Chard' by Miller (1735), other names for this form include 'Large White' and 'Spinach Beet', and in French 'Poirée à Carde'. It is also the 'Italian Beete' of Parkinson (1629), who stated that it 'is of much respect, whose faire greene leaves are very large and great, with great white ribbes and veines therein'. At the end of the 17th century the celebrated naturalist John Ray (1627–1705) in his *Historia Plantarum* (1686) offers the additional synonyms 'Sicilian Broad-Leaved Beet' and *Beta italica*, again suggesting that Swiss chard may originate from Sicily.

Parkinson also records a second, red form, which he describes as the 'great red Beete that Master Lete a Merchant of London gave unto Master Gerrard, as he setteth it downe in his Herball', adding Gerard's comments about the size of the ribs and its culinary worth (quoted above). This may be a precursor of 'Rhubarb' chard (syn. 'Ruby'), which has rhubarb-pink stems and curled, dark green leaves and was in cultivation by 1856. Gerard also says: 'seedes taken from that plant which was altogether of one colour and sowen, doth bring foorth plants of many and variable colours'. This may be an early reference to what is now the cultivar 'Five-coloured' or 'Rainbow Chard', which has stem colours of orange, pink, red, white and yellow, and green or red leaves, and which, in an unexplainable geographical reference, is called 'Brazilian Beet' by *The Gardeners' Chronicle* in 1844. Lastly, and according to M'Intosh (1855), the 'White or Sicilian Beet' was native to that island but was introduced to England in 1570 from Portugal.

OPPOSITE *'Rainbow Chard', 'Rhubarb' chard and 'Swiss Chard'.*

PUMPKIN & SQUASH

Cucurbita maxima, C. mixta, C. moshcata & C. pepo

From an edible perspective the two most significant genera within the family Cucurbitaceae are *Cucumis*, to which melons (see p. 190) and cucumbers (see p. 98) belong, and *Cucurbita*, into which fall courgettes and marrows (see p. 101), pumpkins and squash. And within the genus *Cucurbita* the great diversity of gourd-like fruits are scattered among four species: *C. maxima, C. mixta, C. moschata* and *C. pepo.* Confusingly, the characteristics of individual cultivars do not clearly indicate to which species they belong; moreover, the vernacular terms 'pumpkin' and 'squash' are randomly applied to cultivars of all four species.

Two shared characteristics of the four species are that they are native to Latin America and are ancient crops. *C. maxima* is one of the most diverse of any domesticated species: native to South America, the earliest evidence of its cultivation dates to *c.* 1800 BC and the Virú Valley of Peru. *C. mixta* was in cultivation in the Tehuacan Valley, Puebla, in Mexico, before 5200 BC. *C. moschata* was also domesticated in Latin America, although exactly where is unclear; the oldest archaeological remains were found in the caves of Ocampo, Tamaulipas, in northwestern Mexico and date to 4900 BC. For the ancestry of *C. pepo* see p. 101.

The etymology of the different cultivars is equally bewildering. Suffice to say that 'squash' derives from names given to the fruits by Native Americans, for example *askutasquas* and *souotaersquasties*, while pumpkin is the Americanization of the English 'pompion' ('pompon' or 'pumpion', as Mistress Ford says in Shakespeare's *The Merry Wives of Windsor*), which itself derived originally from *pepon*, the ancient Greek for large melon. In the early literature there was a general distinction between squashes, which fruited in summer, and pumpkins which were an autumn harvest.

Every explorer and adventurer who landed in the New World from Columbus onwards encountered these cucurbits and almost all commented on their profusion. Beginning with Columbus, different types arrived in Europe, and unlike some other New World introductions including the tomato and potato, these vegetables quickly found their way on to the dining table. The chronicler Ralph Holinshed (d. 1580?) noted in 1548 that 'melons' and 'pompions' were eaten as 'deintie dishes at the table of delicate merchants, gentlemen and the nobilitie who make their provision yearlie for new seeds out of strange countries'. The new arrivals also occupied the herbalists and authors of the second half of the 16th century, including of course Gerard. His *Herball* (1597) contains seven illustrations of pumpkins and a range of squash he calls gourds. In the second edition (1633) there is also a long description dedicated to the 'Virginian macock or pompion'. This is believed to be the same cultivar as illustrated by Tragus in 1552 and (re-) introduced in 1881 as 'Perfect Gem Squash'. Still available as 'Gem Squash', it is thus possible to grow one of the earliest introduced squash.

Despite enthusiastic beginnings, a fact acknowledged by M'Intosh in 1855 is that British gardeners have never been as keen on growing and consuming pumpkins and squash as their American cousins. Certainly, these curious cucurbits did not catch the imagination of wealthy garden owners in the way melons and cucumbers did. Indeed, it appears that the pumpkin was cultivated primarily by the poor, for M'Intosh observes that it was grown in England 'where pumpkin-pies are much relished by the peasantry, who store the fruit … for winter use'.

For the dedicated enthusiast a huge range of heirloom varieties can be grown. A long time favourite for pies is 'Small Sugar' (by 1860), while for a bigger pumpkin, 'Rouge Vif d'Etampes' (syn. 'Cinderella') has been cultivated in France since the 1830s; the fruits can reach 6.8 kg (15 lb). If size is an issue, an English cultivar dating to before 1824 is 'Hundred Weight' (syn. 'Mammoth'). Even larger is 'Atlantic Giant'; as of 2011 the record weight stands at 824.8 kg (1,818.5 lb).

After being hugely popular in the mid-19th century, ornamental squash are back in fashion, but there are also many winter squash that not only look interesting but also taste great. Introduced in the 1890s 'Delicata' has a fine-textured, light orange flesh. 'Green Hubbard' was in cultivation by 1842 and originated in Marblehead, Massachusetts, from a single seed. 'Blue Hubbard' probably arrived in the same town from South America sometime in the 18th century; a smaller version is 'Blue Ballet'. Producing fruits up to 9 kg (20 lb), with deep orange flesh which is dense and sweet, 'Muscade de Provence' originated in this area of France in the 19th century. At the small end of the scale 'Patty Pan' is a summer squash famous for its small round fruits flattened in shape with scalloped edges. Said to date from the 1890s and to be from Japan, 'Spaghetti' (syn. 'Vegetable Spaghetti') produces fruits up to 3.2 kg (7 lb). When cooked, the flesh inside turns into spaghetti-like strands. 'Table Queen' is a green-skinned acorn type of squash with fruits that weigh up to 1.3 kg (3 lb). Although introduced in 1913, its pedigree is much older, for not only was this a premier home-steading cultivar, but it was bred from squash grown by Native Americans. For something more decorative, and in cultivation by 1817, 'Turks Turban' (syn. 'Turks Cap') is easily recognized by its unusual shape.

OPPOSITE *Pumpkins and squashes come in a huge variety of shapes, sizes and colours; at the back is 'Atlantic Giant'.* OVERLEAF *'Muscade de Provence', 'Table Queen', 'Turk's Turban', 'Spaghetti', 'Blue Ballet' and 'Pink Banana'.*

SOLANACEAE

The family Solanaceae is very varied and includes many useful and favourite vegetables such as the tomato and potato. The aubergine, or egg-plant, is from the Old World, and chilli, in all its forms, is from the New, but both need heat and a long season to fruit well and thus benefit from being grown under glass.

AUBERGINE OR EGG-PLANT
Solanum melongena

The name aubergine is French, derived from the Catalan *albergínia*, the Arabic *al-badinjan*, the Persian *badin-gan* and finally the Sanskrit *vatin-ganah*. A native to India, and botanically classified as a berry, the aubergine has been cultivated in southern and eastern Asia for millennia. The first written reference has been traced to 59 BC in the text *Tong Yue* by Wang Bao, and indicates that a cultivated form was being grown, and it is also mentioned in other early Chinese sources including the agricultural text *Qi Min Yao Shu* ('Main techniques for the welfare of the people') in AD 544. It is, however, absent from Classical texts, and so was probably brought west later, by Arab traders and conquerors. It was known in Egypt by the 9th century and to the Persian polymath Ibn Sina (Avicenna, d. 1037), who called it *badingan*. The aubergine was in Spain by 1080, when the great botanist of Toledo, Ibn Bassal, wrote about it (by the late 15th century Toledo was renowned for its aubergines). It may have travelled as far north as Germany in the succeeding two centuries, coming to the attention of Albertus Magnus, who refers to the *melangena*.

By the mid-16th century the aubergine was familiar on both sides of the Channel and appears in most of the key texts. Tragus (1552) says it had recently reached Germany from Naples, and Lyte (1578), who calls it the 'Amorous or Raging love apple', is emphatic that the fruit was 'an unwholsome meate, ingendzing the body full of evill humours', adding that the two forms, white- and purple-fruiting, were only grown by 'Herboristes'. Gerard (1597) adds both another name, 'Madde Apples', and a yellow-coloured form. Parkinson (1629) also advises against consuming what was in his time an egg-shaped fruit rather than the elongated form which we are familiar with today (although egg-shaped aubergines are once more being marketed as 'new').

In 1731 Miller is still using the common name 'madde apples', stating that the fruit is not eaten and is grown only for ornament. However, in 1782 Mawe makes no reference to 'madde apples', but does recommend planting the 'egg-plant' as an unusual tender annual. By 1825 another shift has taken place, for Loudon, who also calls it the egg-plant, includes it in the section on 'Plants used as Preserves and Pickles', suggesting it was by now being consumed. Yet even as late as the mid-19th century M'Intosh (1855) relegates the 'aubergine' (one of the first references to the French name) and the tomato to the status of 'Miscellaneous Vegetables'. He also adds a red form to the list of fruit colours, and while acknowledging that the fruits are 'wholesome and excellent food', and popular in France, he says that those who cultivate it in Britain do so only for its novel ornamental value.

Heritage varieties that remain in cultivation include the early 19th-century 'Early Long Purple', which is mentioned by Claude Tollard in his *Traité des végétaux* (1805) and described in 1826 as 'often straight but generally slightly bent; when mature, of a deep purple, but subject to some difference of colour'. 'Imperial Black Beauty' was in cultivation by 1875, its fruits described as 'broad, thick, of most attractive form & finest flavour'; and 'De Barbentane' (by 1897) is a 'productive & early variety, with long slim fruits. Smooth purple skin, covering a firm & tasty flesh'.

OPPOSITE *Aubergine 'Imperial Black Beauty'.*

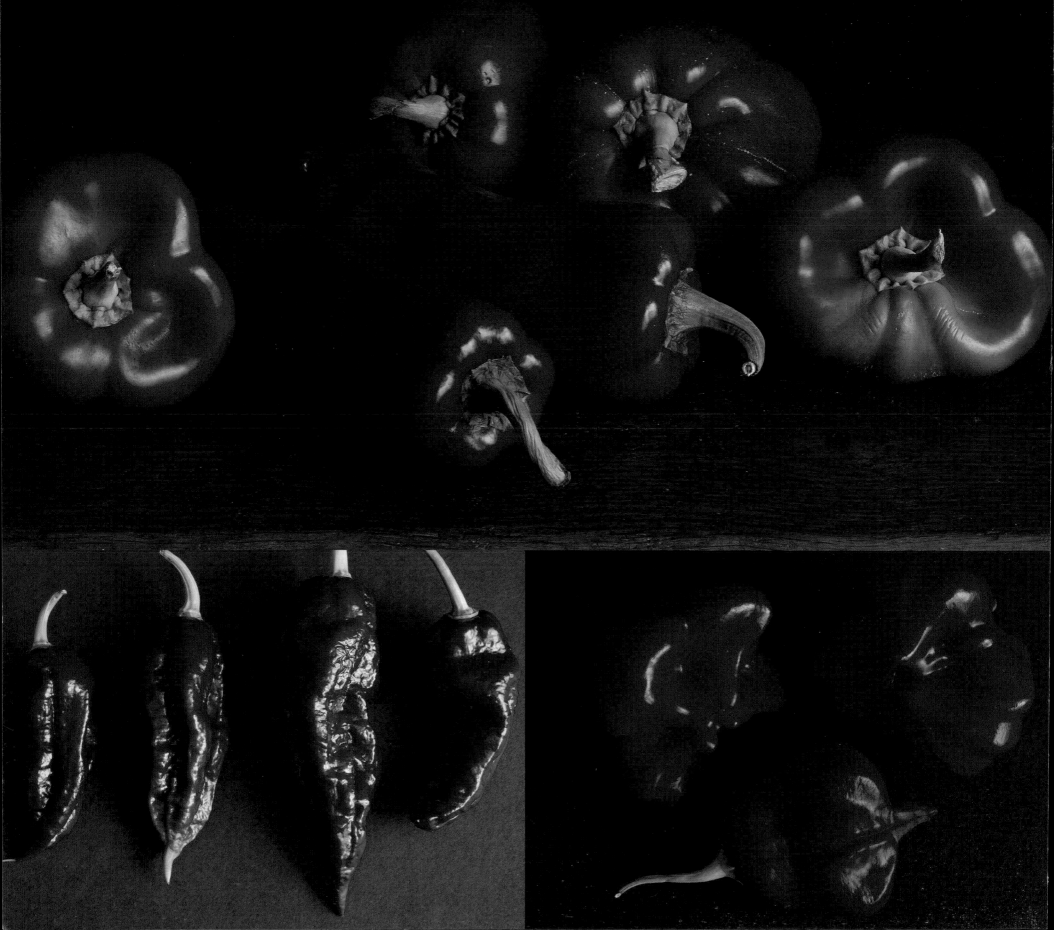

After [the flowers] growe the cods, greene at the first, and when they be ripe of a brave colour glittering like red corall, in which is conteined little flat seedes … of a hot biting taste like common pepper, as is also the cod itself: which is long, and as bigge as a finger and sharpe pointed.

Gerard, 1597

SOLANACEAE

CHILLI & SWEET PEPPER

Capsicum annuum, C. baccatum, C. chinense, C. frutescens, C. pubescens

Native to South and Central America, the genus *Capsicum* contains about 25 species, five of which are important edibles: *C. annuum, C. baccatum, C. chinense, C. frutescens* and *C. pubescens*. The word 'chilli' derives from the Nahuatl word *xilli* and each of the *Capsicum* species contains hot cultivars which may generically be called 'chillis'. The chilli was among the first plants to be domesticated in Central America, with archaeological evidence from southwestern Ecuador showing chillies were being consumed as early as 7500 BC. Archaeologists consider that today's *C. chinense* 'Black Habanero' is the closest to these original fruits.

The species *C. annuum* contains both the mild sweet or bell pepper and much hotter types, for instance cayennes and jalapeños. The main substance that gives chillis their heat is a chemical called capsaicin, and the strength of individual cultivars is measured in Scoville Heat Units (SHU). At one end of the scale is the sweet pepper, with zero SHU, while moving up the scale an average jalapeño contains between 3,000 and 6,000 SHU. The title of hottest is fiercely contested and changes hands frequently, but one recent world record holder is 'Bhut Jolokia' (an interspecific hybrid), which measured a scalding 855,000 SHU.

The chilli is first mentioned by Peter Martyr in a letter dated September 1493, in which he says Columbus brought home 'pepper more pungent than that from Caucasus' (referring to pepper of the genus *Piper*). It may have been Diego Álvarez Chanca, a physician to Columbus's first expedition, who brought the chilli to Spain: he wrote about its medicinal effects in 1494. A century later Gerard says many varieties of the 'ginny' or 'ginnie pepper' are grown and that it had arrived in England from Spain and Italy. John Evelyn cautiously but enthusiastically emphasizes the 'superlatively hot and burning' characteristics of the 'Indian, or Solanum Capsicum' pepper in his *Acetaria* (1699), and Mawe (1779) lists seven types of 'Capsicum', including the 'bell shaped'. By the mid-19th century the chilli was both garden grown and extensively cultivated by market gardeners around London, with the fruits 'maked into pickles and seasonings', and sent 'to supply the Italian warehouses'. Was Britain at this stage exporting chillies to Italy?

Cultivars of *C. annuum* that produce hot fruits include 'Long Red Cayenne', a very early introduction and in cultivation by 1542. The cultivar 'de Comidia' (syn 'Guajillo'), meaning 'Pepper of Food', is of a medium heat with fruits reaching to 20 cm (8 in.) long. Of Brazilian origin and from the species *C. baccatum*, 'Bishop's Cap Red' is an Andean Aji type which produces very unusually shaped fruits of medium heat. At the cool end of the spectrum 'Friggitello' is the classic Italian cultivar that produces great quantities of sweet, tapered fruits up to 10 cm (4 in.) long that turn bright red when ripe. Another Italian classic is 'Long Red Marconi'; in cultivation by 1880 it produces 'Long thin red pods with a sweet flavour. Mild & very productive'. 'California Wonder' is a favourite American heirloom sweet pepper.

OPPOSITE: ABOVE *Sweet peppers 'California Wonder' and 'Long Red Marconi' (centre);* BELOW LEFT *chilli pepper 'Bhut Jolokia';* BELOW RIGHT *chilli pepper 'Bishop's Cap Red'.*

Much of the ease and happiness of the people of the United States is ascribable to the absence of grinding taxation; but that absence alone, without the cultivation of Indian Corn, would not … have created a powerful nation … This plant is the great blessing of the country.

Cobbett, 1831

SWEET CORN
Zea mays convar. *saccharata* var. *rugosa*

The name maize derives from either the indigenous Taíno word *maiz* or the Arawak word *mahiz*. The wild plant (*Zea mays*) has a leafy stalk that produces ears composed of kernels, which are technically a fruit. Full of carbohydrate, the kernels were used as a grain by the indigenous peoples of Mesoamerica, who domesticated maize in prehistoric times. Several complex theories attempt to explain the mechanisms of domestication, but in summary the process is thought to have begun as far back as 10,000 BC in the lowlands of the Balsas River valley in south central Mexico, and remains of maize ears have been found in the Guilá Naquitz Cave in the Oaxaca Valley dating to *c.* 4250 BC. Around 1500 BC maize cultivation spread fast and far – it was introduced to different cultures, new cultivars were bred and varied uses found for it. To give but a single example of how highly regarded maize was, one Quiché Maya word for maize is *kana*, meaning 'our mother'. A traditional method of cultivation is known as 'The Three Sisters', in which maize, beans and squash are grown together: the beans fix nitrogen, thus improving the soil, and are supported by the corn, while the squash covers the ground and suppresses weeds.

Columbus's men encountered this new vegetable on Cuba in 1492, but whether it returned to Europe on this or Columbus's second voyage is unclear. Whenever it made the journey, maize quickly became a garden novelty and equally rapidly spread through France, Italy, southeastern Europe and North Africa. This diffusion may explain why in 1548 Turner, while confirming it was widely grown in Italy and in some German gardens, calls maize 'turkish wheat'. Gerard (1597) also gives it the name 'Turkie Wheate' as well as 'Turkie Corne' and 'Corne of Asia', but does recognize the plant's correct provenance. Yet maize does not appear in English gardening monographs, and when planted by land owners as a field crop was widely considered to be inferior to the traditional cereals already in cultivation. If maize was cultivated at all it was for cattle feed or on a small scale by the poor – the Italian staple *polenta* for example was a mush of ground corn and water. However, William Cobbett, the opinionated English farmer and writer, was an advocate for growing what he called Indian Corn and a firm believer in its advantages, even publishing *A Treatise on Cobbett's Corn* (2nd ed., 1831).

Sweet corn occurs as a spontaneous mutation of maize – the kernels having a higher sugar content and a paler colour. It was known and grown by several Native American tribes. The Iroquois of what is now up-state New York gave the first recorded sweet corn (called *papoon*) to European settlers in 1779. In the 19th century open-pollinated cultivars of white corn became available in the United States, and today the only cultivar of so-called shoepeg corn, characterized by small, narrow kernels tightly and unevenly packed on the cob, is 'Country Gentleman'. Introduced in *c.* 1890 by Frank Woodruff & Sons it was described in 1896 as 'Without doubt the sweetest and most tender of all sweet corns'.

Sweet corn breeding continued in the 20th century and Fred Ashworth, a farmer and plant breeder who established St Lawrence Nurseries in Potsdam in the northernmost part of New York State in the 1920s, was responsible for many new cultivars, including the early ripening 'Ashworth Sweet Corn'. According to FEDCO Seeds, Fred originally named this yellow, sweet-tasting corn 'Rat Selected' because he followed the advice of the rodents that broke into his seed store and selected the type they enjoyed most.

OPPOSITE *'Ashworth Sweet Corn'*.

TURNIP

Brassica rapa var. *rapa*

The turnip or white turnip is a member of the radish, mustard and the cabbage tribe – the genus *Brassica*. It is cultivated across temperate climates for both its leaves ('turnip tops') and root. The mature turnip sits half in and half out of the soil. With a pink- or green-coloured skin, the upper half is botanically speaking a swollen part of the stem, while the below ground half is a white-skinned swollen taproot. When peeled, the flesh is white throughout and the two halves of this usually globular vegetable are indistinguishable.

Although the turnip has not been well preserved in the archaeological record, based on the evidence of the range of the wild turnip (*B. rapa*) and its relatives, together with the etymology of its name, it is suggested that it was domesticated somewhere in west Asia and/or Europe. It was cultivated in antiquity and in the 7th century BC the Greek poet Sappho calls one of her paramours *gongýla* or turnip. Many people may not rate the turnip all that highly these days, but Pliny was far more enthusiastic, placing it third in importance after cereals and beans. He also discusses its cultivation as livestock fodder, a practice that continues to this day, with farmers planting the larger, coarser-fleshed cultivars.

The turnip arrived in Britain with the Romans, and it was a crop that according to archaeologists experienced mixed fortunes, increasing and then decreasing in popularity through the Roman period. The same fate overtook the parsnip, apple and pear. However, it appears that the turnip remained in cultivation after the Romans left. It is the *naep* of the *Læcboc of Bald* and the *aenglisene naep* of the *Lacnunga*. On the continent the turnip is mentioned in documents from the rule of Charlemagne, but is not included in the *Capitulare de Villis*. Albertus Magnus names the turnip in the 13th century and it was an important staple in the centuries before the arrival and acceptance of the potato. In Tudor times the roots were baked or roasted in the ashes of fires as well as boiled or mashed. Turner (1548) differentiates between the 'rape' which 'hath a round roote' and the 'turnepe' also known as the 'navet' and 'navet gentle', which is described as having 'a longe roote and somthynge yealowishe'.

Gerard (1597) depicts the globular 'Great Turnep' and discusses two small forms that have various coloured roots – red, white, green, yellow – all of which are 'sweeter in taste'. He concludes that the 'small Turnep groweth by a village neere London (called Hackney) in a sandie ground, and brought to the Crosse in Cheap-side by the women of that village to be sold … are the best that ever I tasted'. Gerard also discusses the 'naveew-gentle', which was a type of turnip cultivated on the continent, including France and Bavaria, for its seeds, from which an oil was extracted for lamps and soap. Two-and-a-half centuries later M'Intosh (1855) states that the 'French turnip or *navet*' was widely consumed on the continent as it had once been in England, and that it must not be peeled before cooking for its 'particular flavour is in the outer rind'.

However, the turnip's finest hour came in the 18th century. In 1730 Charles Townshend, 2nd Viscount Townshend, retired from politics – like many others he had fallen out with his brother-in-law Sir Robert Walpole – to his estate of Raynham Hall in Norfolk. Here he passed his remaining years as an agricultural improver, playing a significant and lasting role in the British Agricultural Revolution, not least for his introduction of the four-field crop rotation system. He earned the epithet 'Turnip' for his extensive plantings of the root, using seed brought from

OPPOSITE *Turnip 'Golden Ball'.*

ABOVE *Turnip 'Green Top Stone'*. OPPOSITE *Turnip 'Noir d'Hiver'*.

Holland. He also demonstrated that the turnip was the perfect winter fodder for livestock – both nutritious and inexpensive it enabled livestock to be over-wintered rather than killed in the autumn.

An 'early Dutch white' is one of the types about which Mawe offers cultural advice in 1782, another is 'French, small round', which may be one of the ones Gerard was so enamoured with. In M'Intosh's opinion, improved garden cultivars were imported from Holland and Flanders from Tudor times onwards, and the cultivars named by Mawe would seem to confirm that new cultivars did not appear in Britain during the second half of the 18th century. M'Intosh adds that 'Swedish turnip' or rutabaga (*B. napobrassica*) was particularly valuable in colder areas, and had been introduced to Scotland in 1781 or 1782 from Gothenburg in Sweden.

Of the heritage varieties available, 'Golden Ball' (syn. 'Orange Jelly') was raised by a Mr Chivas of Chester and was in cultivation by 1838. The roots are globe shaped, amber coloured and 10 cm (4 in.) in diameter, with a fine, firm texture. In cultivation by 1821, 'Green Top Stone' (syn. 'Manchester Market') is perfect for late sowing and will stand in the garden long into the winter. Do not be dissuaded by the unusual appearance of the French cultivar 'Noir d'Hiver'. With a long, cylindrical, black-skinned root, it is just how certain turnips looked in the 16th century and when peeled it has delicious tasting white flesh. Bred by the famous nursery of that name, 'Veitch's Red Globe' was in cultivation by 1838 but acquired its new name in 1868; it produces roots with white, solid flesh with the above-ground skin a beautiful purplish red.

Winter

*Winter is a time of chill and warmth: of sharp, astringent frosts and steaming
manure to be dug into beds. There is a scent of decay in the air, a reminder that the
season is over and the garden is now slumbering. The light is brief, low and pale,
but shafts of sun make the rime of hoarfrost on the brassicas glitter and the cobwebs
sparkle. For the gardener it is a time of calm reflection, looking back over the season
with enjoyment at the successes, and with humility and humour at the lessons learned.
And of course, as the nights draw in it is good to light the fire and sit in comfort,
knowing that the kitchen garden will continue to provide something through the winter
months, to be supplemented by the cornucopia of produce stored and preserved.
And don't forget that bottle of mulberry gin and the pleasure of planning
next season's campaign, when it all begins again.*

HOTHOUSE EXOTICS

Certain fruits will only yield well if provided with the shelter and protection of a heated glasshouse, and while the vine will grow outdoors, it will produce much better if grown inside. From the mid-18th century onwards, growing fruits such as grapes and melons in hothouses was as much about showing that one could – that one had the wealth sufficient for the protective structures and that one's head gardener and garden were up-to-scratch – as it was about the harvest. The aim was to impress and to enjoy the plaudits of being able to serve envious guests with both unusual, exotic fruits and more familiar ones harvested out of season.

GRAPE

Vitis vinifera

The grape is indigenous to the Mediterranean region, extending into central Europe and southwestern Asia. Its fruits would have been harvested by hunter-gatherers and archaeological evidence suggests that the earliest known production of wine occurred in Georgia some 8,000 years ago. But changes in pip shape (narrower in domesticated forms) that appear in the archaeological record of southwest Asia, the south Caucasus (Armenia and Georgia) and the western Black Sea region (Bulgaria) date the domestication of the grape to *c.* 3500–3000 BC. The first written account of the grape is found in the Sumerian *Epic of Gilgamesh* dating from the 3rd millennium BC. From Mesopotamia the grape spread west to Phoenicia and then Egypt, where it was sacred to the goddess Hathor, who embodied fertility and greeted the souls of the dead to the West. An inscription on a jar from as early as the 1st dynasty King Semerkhet (early 3rd millennium BC) names a royal vineyard, and later tomb paintings of ancient Egyptian gardens often show vines, sometimes grown over a large pergola structure to provide both shade and grapes.

The grape has played a central role in cultures and religions everywhere it has been cultivated and fermented. Numerous references are found in the Bible, for instance, including in the ninth chapter of Genesis, where Noah planted a vineyard and 'drank of the wine and was drunken'. In the Book of Deuteronomy the vine is one of the seven types of produce (including the fig) with which the Promised Land of Israel is blessed, and it features also in the New Testament. The first of Jesus' miracles described in John's gospel is turning water into wine at the marriage at Cana, and of himself Jesus said 'I am the true vine' (John 15:1).

The Phoenicians took the grape across the Mediterranean to Greece around 1000 BC and the vine and wine appear repeatedly in *The Odyssey*, including Homer's delightful description of the Mediterranean as the 'wine-dark sea'. It was the ancient Greeks who developed the art of viticulture, believing that wine was a gift from Dionysos (Bacchus in Roman mythology), who had invented it on Mount Nyssa. Dionysos' foster-father, the old satyr Seilenos (or Silenus), was the rustic god of the dance of the wine-press and drunkenness. Greek hangovers must have been rather painful, for the available technology would have produced a vintage of questionable quality and clarity, no doubt warranting Homer's frequent references to diluting wine with water. The Romans took wine production and the principles of viticulture very seriously, and

OPPOSITE *Grapes 'Schiava Grossa' (above left) and 'Alicante' (above right and in bowl).*

The grapes of the best sorts of Vines are pressed into wine by some in these dayes with us, and much more I verily believe in times past, as by the name of Vineyard given to many places in this Kingdome, especially where Abbies and Monasteries stood, may bee coniectured: but the wine of late made hath beene but small, and not durable, like that which cometh from beyond Sea, whether our unkindly yeares or the want of skill, or a convenient place for a Vineyard be the cause, I cannot well tell you.

Parkinson, 1629

both Cato and Pliny wrote at length about the vine. Cato offers cultural advice and Pliny lists 91 varieties of grape and 50 kinds of wine. Indeed, the world's oldest surviving vintage is claimed to be from AD 325, in an amphora discovered inside a sarcophagus in Speyer in Germany.

In the centuries following the withdrawal of the Roman legions from Britain it was the monasteries that preserved the art of viticulture. In his *Historia ecclesiastica gentis Anglorum* (Ecclesiastical History of the English People), completed in 731, the Venerable Bede makes references to vine cultivation; and by medieval times clergy, royalty and nobility were all actively cultivating vines. Compiled in 1086, Domesday Book lists as major taxable assets 38 vineyards in the southern counties: the grapes of Gloucestershire were particularly renowned for their sweetness and the quality of the wine produced. By 1229 the famous vineyard at Ely covered some 6.5 ha (16 acres) and the Keeper was receiving 10½ pence per week, together with an annual robe (suit of clothes). And in one unfortunate connection, the name of George Plantagenet, 1st Duke of Clarence, is remembered as the character in Shakespeare's *Richard III* who is drowned in a butt of Malmsey wine, a sweet wine traditionally from Madeira.

Vines and grapes never fell from fashion, although cultivation suffered a decline from the 14th to the 17th century, the result of a combination of climatic change – the end of the Medieval Warm Period and from 1550 the start of the Little Ice Age – and the Black Death, which led to a shortage of a skilled rural workforce. The revival of the grape came with its moving indoors under the cover of the glasshouse.

In 1629 Parkinson listed 23 types of grape including 'The white Muscadine Grape', which is a 'verie great Grape, sweete and firme, some of the bunches have weighed six pound, and some of the grapes halfe an ounce'. Today, the white cultivar 'Muscat of Alexandria' has literally dozens of synonyms including 'Chasselas Musqué'. Wine experts believe it is one of the oldest genetically unmodified vines still in existence and legend has it that the pharaoh Cleopatra drank Muscat wine produced in Greece. As a table grape this cultivar produces medium-sized round grapes with a pale amber skin; the flesh is juicy with a rich, sweet, Muscat flavour. Included by Thomas Hitt in his *A Treatise of Fruit-trees* (1757) is Britain's most famous historic grape cultivar, 'Schiava Grossa' (syn. 'Black Hamburgh'), which is vigorous, easy to cultivate and annually produces a heavy harvest of large bunches of dark red or purple grapes. This cultivar is the Great Vine at Hampton Court palace, planted in 1768 by the Royal Gardener, Lancelot 'Capability' Brown (1716–83), which continues to produce a crop of about 270 kg (600 lb) of grapes every year.

Another valuable heritage variety of more recent origin is 'Alicante' (syn. 'Alicante Bouschet'), which was bred between 1865 and 1885 by Henri Bouschet from his father's crossing of 'Petit Bouschet' with 'Grenache' and was an immediate success.

OPPOSITE *Grape 'Muscat of Alexandria'.*

HOTHOUSE EXOTICS

MUSKMELON
Cucumis melo

According to Léon de Fos in his collection of proverbs and aphorisms, *Gastronomiana* (1870), three things that cannot support mediocrity are poetry, wine and melons. But 'melon' is one of those generic names that causes all sorts of confusion: what exactly is the difference between a muskmelon, a honeydew and a cantaloupe? In fact they are all just variations on a theme. The muskmelon is the species native to Persia, Armenia and the trans-Caucasus region that has been bred to produce many different cultivars. The honeydew is a cultivar group, *Cucumis melo* Inodorus, and 'Honeydew' is the American name for the cultivar 'White Antibes', which has been grown for the longest time in the south of France and Algeria. The cantaloupe, which gets its name from the former papal estate of Cantaluppi near Rome, is *Cucumis melo* var. *cantalupensis* and originated in India and North Africa.

Melons are mentioned in the Sumerian *Epic of Gilgamesh* and were among the fruits missed by the Israelites during their 40-year sojourn in the wilderness. Another belief system in which the melon played a significant role was Manichaeism, which arose in Babylon in the 3rd century AD; devotees believed melons aided in the fight of light (good) against dark (evil). Theophrastus mentions melon cultivation, while Dioscorides and Pliny refer to the *pepo* and *melopepo* respectively. However, it is not clear whether the authors are referring to the melon or the watermelon (*Citrullus lanatus*), a native of southern Africa which had reached Egypt by the 2nd millennium BC. In the 4th century Apicius offers a recipe for *pepones et melones*, which could be watermelon with muskmelon.

The word *hwerhwette* in the 10th-century *Læcboc of Bald* refers either to melon or cucumber, but the melon is specifically named by several early authors including Alexander Neckam and Albertus Magnus, suggesting that it was brought across the Channel either by monks in the Dark Ages or in the wake of the Norman Conquest. Also in the 13th century but far to the east, Marco Polo encountered dried melons in Afghanistan, recalling that they were 'the best melons in the world in very great quantity'.

It was not until the mid-16th century that the melon became widely cultivated in England, by which time many authors were using the name *pepo*. Gerard in his *Herball* (1597) describes round, long, oval and pear-shaped forms and mentions places in London, including 'the Queenes house at St James', where he had seen fruits grown successfully. By the 1633 edition of his book, the term 'muske-melon' or 'million' was being used, and musk, sugar and Spanish, and pear-shaped types were described. To produce the best quality fruits in a cooler climate as in Britain, the melon had to be grown on hotbeds, which in later centuries were covered with lights (large cloches). As glasshouse design evolved from the late 18th century onwards, the melon was provided with its own specially designed hothouse.

New cultivars were also developed, and by 1855 M'Intosh could recommend 24 different melons including Gerard's 'Spanish'. However, not on his list was 'Early Black Rock' (syn. 'Noir des Carmes'), which is listed by Mawe in 1787 but may be an even older French cultivar bred by Carmelite monks. Cut open its very dark green skin and the surprise is the beautifully sweet orange flesh. Bred in 1880 by Thomas Crump, head gardener to the Duke of Marlborough at Blenheim Palace in Oxfordshire, 'Blenheim Orange' was offered by the seed merchant Carters from 1897. With slightly 'netted' skin, bright orange flesh and a fantastic sweet flavour, this cultivar is generally glasshouse-grown but also has good cold tolerance. Of French origin and with a warty skin 'Prescott Fond Blanc' was in cultivation by 1850 but is also probably much older. The refined cantaloupe 'Charentais' is considered by many to be the finest of all melons. Round and with a smooth, creamy grey skin, its orange flesh is sweet, juicy and has a delightful fragrance. This very special cultivar originated in the Poitou-Charentes region of France in *c.* 1920.

OPPOSITE *Melons 'Prescott Fond Blanc', 'Blenheim Orange' (sliced), 'Early Black Rock' and 'Charentais' (left to right).*

I first saw yᵉ famous Queen Pine brought from Barbados and presented to his Maᵗⁱᵉ; but the first that were ever seen in England were those sent to Cromwell foure years since.

Evelyn, 1661

HOTHOUSE EXOTICS

PINEAPPLE
Ananas comosus

The word 'pineapple' dates to 1398 when it was used to describe the productive organs (cones) of the pine tree (*Pinus* spp.). A century later, in November 1493, Christopher Columbus had the first European encounter with what we today call the pineapple when he landed on Guadeloupe. The pineapple is native to tropical South America, in particular Brazil and Colombia, and the genus name *Ananas* derives from 'nanas', the Tupian word meaning 'excellent fruit' (as recorded by André Thevet in 1555 in what is now Brazil); *comosus* means, aptly, 'tufted'.

Considering the pineapple requires hot, humid, tropical conditions to produce fruit, it made surprisingly rapid progress in finding new homes in which it could thrive. Two years after Columbus's encounter it was growing on St Helena, and by 1548 had travelled as far east as India. However, the pineapple's introduction to and spread across Europe is somewhat unclear. The first published description appeared in Spain in 1535 and there is a 1592 account from the Dutch botanist Bernhard Paludanus recording his failure to cultivate a pineapple at Enkhuizen.

In England, John Evelyn wrote that the first pineapples in the country were those sent to Oliver Cromwell in 1657, and he himself saw the single fruit sent from Barbados to Charles II in 1661. However, the meticulous Evelyn does not mention pineapples being cultivated in England. This absence, together with the fact that the fruit is difficult to grow, makes it unlikely that the example shown in Hendrick Danckerts's painting (*c.* 1677) being presented to Charles II was the first pineapple cultivated in England, but rather an imported fruit. What is fact is that an English-raised fruit was presented to Charles's niece, Queen Mary II, in 1693 from a plant growing in her glasshouses at Hampton Court palace. Where the parent plant had come from is unknown, but an educated guess – given the glasshouses were erected specifically to house over

400 exotics that accompanied Mary from Holland – is that it was part of her collection. An alternative explanation is that plants were shipped direct from the Indies.

Throughout the 18th and 19th centuries the pineapple was *the* fruit to grow and exhibit if you wished to demonstrate your (or, more accurately, your head gardener's) horticultural expertise and prowess. The king of pineapple cultivation in the 18th century was Henry Telende, head gardener at Pembroke Villa on Richmond Green, London, and his 19th-century counterpart was James 'Barnes of Bicton', who in 1842 managed to raise a mighty 'Queen Pine' of 2.78 kg. (6 lb 2 oz). Before the mid-19th century development of piped hot-water heating systems, accepted wisdom was to raise pineapples in a 'pinery' – essentially a brick-lined pit covered with glass lights within which the potted plants were plunged into a depth of fermenting tanners bark that acted as the heat source. It was exactly the complexities of pineapple cultivation combined with the advent of both the canning process and speedy refrigerated shipping that sounded the death knell for pineapple cultivation in Britain in the early 20th century. However, there has been a small renaissance, with a number of restored 19th-century pineries once again producing. For example, at the Lost Gardens of Heligan in Cornwall the cultivars 'Jamaica Queen' and 'Smooth Cayenne' are grown. The exact introduction date of 'Smooth Cayenne' is not known, but it appears in M'Intosh's 'Select List' of 29 cultivars in *The Book of the Garden* (1855). So-named because it has few or no spines and originates from Cayenne in what is now French Guiana, 'Smooth Cayenne' remains one of the most popular commercially grown cultivars.

OPPOSITE *A young pineapple from Heligan.*

PINEAPPLE | WINTER   193

BRASSICAS

*For centuries, the winter brassicas were an important leafy vegetable crop that helped sustain both rich and poor through the long lean months. In earliest times only the wild cabbage (*Brassica oleracea*) was available, but as selection and domestication continued over the centuries so the range of winter greens increased, though two of the four we cultivate today are relative newcomers – broccoli and Brussels sprouts.*

BROCCOLI
Brassica oleracea Italica Group

Broccoli is an Italian word derived from the Latin *brachium* meaning an arm or branch, and as the name suggests this brassica is a vegetable of Italy. The selection and development that resulted in broccoli occurred specifically in central and southern Italy and Sicily. Pliny wrote about a plant he called *cyma*, which fits the description of broccoli, and some think it is identifiable in Apicius' *De Re Coquinaria*, but its precise date of domestication remains unknown.

Two main divisions of broccoli are heading and sprouting. Heading broccoli is the type that forms a curd on top of a stalk and is reminiscent of cauliflower (see p. 27). Sprouting broccoli make a branching cluster of flower buds on top of a thick stem, with smaller clusters arising along it from the leaf axils (the junction where the main stem meets the leaf stem or petiole). The earliest description, if not Pliny, is made by Jacques Daléchamps in his *Historia generalis plantarum* (1586). Evelyn (1699) mentions 'the Broccoli from Naples', and sprouting broccoli is probably what Miller refers to in his *The Gardeners' Dictionary* (1731) as 'sprout colliflower' or 'Italian asparagus'. According to Miller this novelty arrived in England in 1719.

In 1729 Stephen Switzer reported cultivating several types from a mixed batch of seed, and from his descriptions it seems likely he was growing both sprouting and heading. In the 1768 edition of his *Dictionary* Miller names several forms including 'Roman' or 'Purple', 'Neapolitan' or 'White', and 'Black'. In the early part of the 19th century John Claudius Loudon expounds on the history of the broccoli in Britain, saying that the 'few broccolis … known in Miller's time are supposed to have proceeded from the cauliflower, which was originally imported from the Isle of Cyprus, about the middle of the 16th century. Miller mentions the white and purple broccoli as coming from Italy; and it is conjectured, that from these two sorts all the subsequent kinds have arisen, either by accidental or premeditated impregnations.' By the middle of the same century, M'Intosh describes 10 'approved sorts' of broccoli, together with cultural advice, indicating that it was a popular crop at that time.

A few heritage varieties remain available, including the perennially popular 'Purple Sprouting', which is mentioned in 1777; and from the same date is 'Early White Sprouting' – these may also be the types described by Miller. Another early cultivar is 'Italian Green Sprouting', which is described in 1784 as 'A distinct variety forming good-sized green heads'. Broccoli 'Purple Cape' was certainly discussed by 1830 as a fine variety, while 'Nine Star Perennial' was offered by 1927 as a broccoli that 'each plant of which will give a crop of from 5 to 15 heads of good saleable size & of excellent quality year after year'.

OPPOSITE *Broccoli 'Purple Sprouting'*.

The sprouts are used as winter greens; and at Brussels they are
sometimes served at table with a sauce composed of vinegar, butter,
and nutmeg, poured upon them hot after they have been boiled.
The top, Van Mons says, is very delicate when dressed,
and quite different in flavor from the sprouts.

Loudon, 1825

BRASSICAS

BRUSSELS SPROUT

Brassica oleracea Gemmifera Group

No prizes for guessing its place of origin, but it may be a surprise to learn that the perennially popular (to some) Brussels sprout entered the British garden as recently as the early 19th century. The first English author to discuss it appears to be Loudon in his *An Encyclopaedia of Gardening* (1825). Loudon quotes a paper read by a Van Mons before the (Royal) Horticultural Society in 1818, saying that 'Brussels is noted for the greens or sprouts, which bear the name of that town' and that they 'are mentioned in the market regulations of that city so early as 1213'. The legend that the Brussels sprout was introduced by a Roman legionary would certainly fit with the pattern of other cultivated brassicas originating in the southern and eastern Mediterranean region and then moving north via Italy. However, the fact that Loudon proceeds to offer cultural advice by quoting another source suggests that the sprout was in cultivation in Britain only by the early 1820s. Why the sprout took 600 years to travel from Brussels to Britain has not been established. One possible explanation is that the morphology of the sprout itself confused matters. The vegetable is technically a leaf bud that develops in the leaf axil, but a true cabbage will produce similar buds if the head is removed. It is this post-decapitation phenomenon that may have led Daléchamps (1586) to classify the Brussels sprout, inaccurately, as a type of cabbage – *Brassica capitata polycephalos* – a classification that subsequently misinformed all 17th-century authors.

The sprout was cultivated throughout the 19th century, but if number of page inches within gardening texts of the time is used as a measure, it was neither popular nor widely grown. Suttons in 1879 offered four cultivars: 'Sutton's Matchless', 'Mein's Victoria', 'Scrymger's Giant' and 'Roseberry'. Unfortunately, few heritage varieties are still available. From 1922 'Bedfordshire Fill Basket' produces 'the largest & most solid sprouts in cultivation. Although the buttons grow to a large size they are of extremely good quality.' From around the same time another cultivar that can still be grown is 'Evesham Special', first listed in 1926. For those who enjoy novelty, 'Rubine' is a red variety, probably introduced in the 1930s, while 'Noisette' is an old French variety that produces small to medium-sized sprouts with a delicious, nutty flavour that can be picked over a long period. Perfect for an exposed location 'Early Half Tall' is compact, early harvesting and prolific, neatly producing from top to bottom of the stalk.

OPPOSITE *Sprouts 'Bedfordshire Fill Basket', 'Early Half Tall', 'Rubine' and 'Noisette' (top to bottom).*

BRASSICAS

CABBAGE

Brassica oleracea Capitata Group

The cabbage is a very useful vegetable, for there are spring and summer maturing types as well as the winter cabbage, of which there are three forms. The red- and green-coloured drumhead both have football-shaped heads composed of tightly packed smooth leaves. The third type, the Savoy, has a looser head composed of crinkled or blistered leaves. It is possible that the wild cabbage was domesticated in Britain before the Romans, but it is far more likely that the cabbage arrived in Britain with them. It was the *caules* in the *Læcboc of Bald* and the *cawlic* in the *Lacnunga,* and it became familiar as the cole or colewort, widely planted and commented on throughout the medieval and Tudor periods.

According to Gerard (1597), Dioscorides 'maketh two kinds of Colewoorts: the tame and the wilde', and he also says that coleworts were known to Theophrastus, Columella and Pliny, who distinguished between the 'ruffed or curled Cole' and the 'smooth Cole'. The latter had smooth broad leaves on a 'bigger stalk', and it is likely that the former is a reference to the Savoy. Evidence for an Italian origin for the Savoy is given by Ruellius, who in his *De natura stirpium* (1536) names a loose-heading cabbage 'Romnanos'. Gerard helpfully adds that eating raw 'Colewoorts' before meat 'doth preserve a man from drunkenness'. By 1830 conical, elliptical and spherical types of Savoy were known.

To form tight heads the cabbage requires cool growing conditions and this explains the drumhead's absence from the ancient texts. The name 'cabbage' may derive from the Norman *caboche*, meaning 'head', or simply from *boche* meaning 'swelling' or 'bump'. Albertus Magnus seems to describe a headed cabbage in the late 13th century, but the first definite description is Ruellius, who calls them 'capucos coles' or 'cabutos'. The first mention of a red cabbage is in *Stirpium Adversaria Nova* (1570) by Matthias de L'Obel and Pierre Pena; and it is mentioned by Gerard.

The latter also describes the cabbage with 'leaves wrapped together into a rounde head or globe, whose head is white of colour especially toward winter when it is ripe'. Cabbage was, he stated, 'commonly eaten all over this kingdome'. And it was not only the usual boiled cabbage that was consumed: Evelyn (1699) says that 'colewort-tops' were regarded as salad and M'Intosh (1855) states that for nutritional reasons a fashion was developing for eating cabbage when young, in the form of 'cabbage plants, or cabbage sprouts'. He also notes that red cabbage was cultivated primarily for pickling. Incidentally, James Cook helped to keep his crew free from scurvy throughout his first circumnavigation (1768–71) by feeding them pickled cabbage – sauerkraut. For the same medical reasons, but perhaps more palatable, was the prophylaxis involving lemon taken by Cook's cabin-mate, the wealthy naturalist Sir Joseph Banks (see p. 53).

Old heritage varieties include Savoy 'Large Drumhead' (by 1771), cabbage 'Brunswick' (before 1800) and red cabbage 'Red Drumhead' (syn. 'Red Dutch', by 1771). Cabbage 'January King' (syn. 'De Pontoise') has 'dense, green, round to slightly flattened heads … attractive, purple-tinged outer leaves' and was in cultivation by 1867; cut in February it was renowned for its extreme hardiness. Cabbage 'Primo' is a popular summer-harvesting cultivar that produces a solid 'ball head'. 'Ormskirk' (syn. 'Irish Giant Drumhead') is 'An extra late green Savoy with crinkled leaves & firm rounded heads' that dates to 1899. It is especially cold tolerant and was harvested for Christmas dinner. Another very hardy Savoy is the famous 'Winter King', which is generally regarded as the finest tasting cabbage, and with its red and burgundy markings on the outer leaves adds ornament to the winter garden.

OPPOSITE *Top row: cabbage 'January King' (left and right) and Savoy 'Winter King' (centre). Bottom row: Savoy 'Ormskirk'.*

ABOVE *Red cabbage 'Marner Lagerrot' (cut) and cabbage 'Langedijker Bewaar' (behind).*

The borecole contains several subvarieties, the common characteristic
of all which is an open head, sometimes large, of curled or wrinkled leaves,
and a peculiar hardy constitution, which enables them to resist the winter,
and remain green and fresh during the season … it is impossible to find
a plant of more excellence for the table, or more easily cultivated.

Loudon, 1825

BRASSICAS

KALE

Brassica oleracea Acephala Group

With its central loose leaves – which may be curled, wrinkled or blistered – forming an open head, kale or borecole (from the Dutch *boerenkool* meaning 'peasant's cabbage') is considered to be the closest of all the domesticated forms to their common ancestor, the wild cabbage (*Brassica oleracea*). However, the exact history of its domestication is not clear. Theophrastus mentions three kinds of flat-leaved *rhaphanos* (*rhaphanos* is kale, *raphanos* is radish): a curly leaved, a smooth-leaved and a wild type. To the Romans these were Sabellian kale, and while both Cato and Pliny make mention of different brassicas, not all are readily identifiable. Cato describes the *levis* (large, broad-leaves and large-stalked), the *crispa* or *apiacan*, and the *lenis* (small-stalked, tender, but rather sharp-tasting), and Pliny describes numerous types, also each with their own name and distinctive characteristics.

The same words used in the earliest English literary sources for cabbage could also mean kale. However, kale is definitely on Charlemagne's 8th-century list of selected plants (*Capitulare de Villis*) and continued to be grown down the centuries as an important winter green. Gerard (1597) includes an illustration of 'Swolen Colewoort', which 'of al [*sic*] other is the strangest… This goodly Colewort hath many leaves of a blewish greene, or of the colour of Woade, bunched or swollen up about the edges as it were a peece of leather wet and broiled on a gridiron'. In 1912 George Henslow quotes a 'Mr. Sutton' (presumably of the seed house), who states that he is 'struck with the close resemblance … to two types of kale which are well known in the trade to-day. One is the *Chou palmier* of France, or palm-tree kale of England [and] the Welsh tree kale'. The former, which remains in cultivation and is known by a range of different names including black cabbage, Tuscan kale, Lacinato and Nero de Toscana, is the cultivar 'Cavolo Nero'. Of Italian origin, it is one of the plants listed by Thomas Jefferson as growing in his garden at Monticello in 1777.

The 19th-century country house vegetable garden saw a surge in popularity in the cultivation of kale, as well as the native sea kale (*Crambe maritima*), which was often forced in sea kale pots. In Scotland kale was such a fundamental component of the diet that 'kail' was used as a generic term for dinner. On the Western Isles most properties had a walled 'kailyard', a term subsequently used disparagingly for a group of late 19th- and early 20th-century Scottish authors including J. M. Barrie, with their sentimental, nostalgic descriptions of rural Scottish life.

In cultivation by 1777 'Dwarf Green Curled' was prized on account of its hardiness: 'The green curl'd is a fine winter food for cattle, no frosts can destroy it, therefore it will supply when Cabbages & Savoys are gone'. A hybrid between a curly scotch kale and thousand-headed kale, 'Pentland Brig' is renowned for its flavour and texture, and for its long season – it produces young crown leaves from November, and in spring leafy side shoots and spears appear that can be picked like broccoli.

OPPOSITE *Kale 'Pentland Brig'.*

ABOVE *Kale 'Dwarf Green Curled'*.

ABOVE *Kale 'Cavolo Nero'.*

There be three sorts of plants comprehended under the title *Cichoreum* or Succorie, that is to saie Chichorie, Endive, & Dandelion, differing not so much in the operation & working, as in shape and forme.

Gerard, 1597

CHICORY
Cichorium intybus

Chicory, succory or radicchio is a native salad leaf that has been consumed for millennia, while more recently the root has been used as an adulterant for coffee. But when chicory was domesticated is not clear. The ancients knew of it – it is the *seris* of the Greeks and the *intubum* of the Romans – but do not describe its cultivation. Similarly, in northern Europe it is mentioned by various authors including Neckam in the 13th century and Turner in the 16th century, who names it succory and 'hardewes'. The first to describe chicory in cultivation was the Flemish botanist Rembert Dodoens (1583), who stated that it occurred wild throughout all Germany but was also grown in gardens. The first English account of cultivation is by John Ray in his *Historia Plantarum* (1686), and chicory subsequently became a winter staple.

Witloof or Belgian chicory looks like a dandelion; it has been cultivated by Belgians and French gardeners for centuries and is a favourite type for forcing. The Victorians dug up plants in autumn and trimmed the roots to 20–22 cm (8 or 9 in.) in length and the leaves to 4 cm (1½ in.) from the neck. The roots were then planted or potted up and kept in a dark, cool place such as the cellar or under a greenhouse bench until the leaves appeared, pale and tender.

The Italians have preserved many heritage varieties of chicory, often with local connections. With very red-tinged green leaves, the classic 'Rossa di Treviso' is a cultivar from the Treviso area that dates to the 18th century. The red colour of the leaves intensifies with winter cold and the midribs turn white. From the same century and country, but from the Castelfranco region of northern Italy, 'Variegata di Castelfranco' is highly decorative, with green leaves blotched with red forming an inner loose head in autumn.

OPPOSITE *Chicory 'Variegata di Castelfranco'.* OVERLEAF *Chicory 'Rossa di Treviso'.*

While upon this subject, it will be as well to speak of the leek …
because [it] has recently acquired considerable celebrity from the
use made of it by the Emperor Nero. That prince, to improve his
voice, used to eat leeks and oil every month, upon stated days.

Pliny, 1st century AD

LEEK
Allium porrum

The wild leek is native to southern Europe and western Asia. Its domesticated form has been selected for a long cylinder of bundled leaf sheaths (rather than a bulb, as in the case of its cousins the onion and garlic), which are generally blanched by earthing-up the soil around them. The leek has been in cultivation in Mesopotamia and Egypt from at least the 2nd millennium BC. Evidence from Egypt shows a leek with long, slender leaves, and it took until *c.* AD 500 before the familiar broad leaf form was in cultivation in Italy. The *prason* of the ancient Greeks and the *porrum* to the Romans, the leek was familiar to all the Classical writers. Pliny, who says the best came from Egypt, recounts how the leek was a favourite vegetable of the emperor Nero, who consumed it in oil, believing it beneficial to the quality of his voice; as a result, according to Gerard, the emperor acquired the nickname *porophagus* or 'leek-eater'.

The Romans introduced the leek to Britain, and it is named as *porleac* and *cropleac* in the *Læcboc of Bald* and *bradleac, holleac* and *porleaces* in the *Lacnunga*. But of course there is a far more famous early historical appearance of the leek. In AD 633 an alliance of Welsh and Mercians joined in battle against the Northumbrians at Heathfield (or Hatfield Chase) in Yorkshire. In order to distinguish friend from enemy, Cadwallon ap Cadfan, the king of Gwynedd, told his troops to pluck a handy leek and wear it in their hats. The legend may be apocryphal (and there are other versions) – though the battle certainly took place – but the leek became forever entwined with Welsh culture and symbolism.

The leek is mentioned in all the medieval texts written in England and the majority on the continent, and other documentary records demonstrate that this vegetable was common fare. Ecclesiastical accounts from 1210–11 show that leek seed was purchased at a cost of 2½ pence for the garden of the Bishop of Winchester's London palace at Southwark. In 1290 one of the responsibilities of the royal gardener at Chester in Cheshire, Edward I's headquarters during his campaign into north Wales, was to secure a sufficient quantity of leeks to last through Lent. And in 1321–22 Roger, gardener to the Archbishop of Canterbury at Lambeth Palace, sowed two *lagen* (pints?) of leek seed costing 2s 8d.

The leek remained in high regard as a staple through the winter months, although Gerard (1597) sounds a note of caution when he says that the leek may 'heateth the bodie, ingendreth naughtie bloud, causeth troublesome and terrible dreames'. In 1726 Benjamin Townsend in *The Complete Seedsman* says that 'Leeks are mightily used in the kitchen for Broths and Sauces', and many others mention their particular use in pottage and soups.

The leek has never lost its popularity and one of the most familiar heritage cultivars is 'Musselburgh', which was raised by James Hardcastle of Musselburgh in East Lothian in Scotland and was in cultivation by 1824. The mild-flavoured 'Prizetaker' is a selection from 'Lyon', and according to *The Garden Magazine* was in cultivation by 1885. It produces 'Stems … a foot long and 5 inches in diameter'. 'Lyon' itself is a Scottish cultivar producing large stems up to 50 cm (20 in.) long, 10 cm (4 in.) in circumference and 2.3 kg (5 lb) in weight. It was introduced prior to 1883 by Stuart & Mein of Kelso and was lauded as 'Unquestionably the finest in existence, being of enormous size, splendid mild flavour, & perfectly hardy'. Of French origin are 'Jaune Gros de Poitou' (by 1853) and 'Monstrueux de Carentan' (by 1874).

OPPOSITE *Leek 'Lyon'.*

Parsnips contain a very considerable portion of sugar, and from this cause they yield a very excellent spirit by distillation. In the north of Ireland the cottagers obtain a sort of beer by mashing the roots and boiling them with hops, and then fermenting the liquor. Wine closely approaching in quality the Malmsey of Madeira is made from the roots.

M'Intosh, 1855

PARSNIP
Pastinaca sativa

The genus *Pastinaca* includes 14 species, one of which is the wild parsnip, native to Britain as well as Eurasia. The name 'parsnip' is derived from the Middle English *pasnepe*, itself descended from the Latin verb *pastino* 'to dig' or *pastinum*, a type of two-pronged dibble or fork. The latter derivation may relate to the forked roots that tend to develop if the parsnip is grown in stony soil. Like its close relative the carrot, the parsnip has not survived in the archaeological record and so it is not possible to establish an exact date of domestication, but the root has been in cultivation at least since antiquity. As mentioned (see p. 94), there is a general lack of clarity among Classical authors when discussing the parsnip and carrot. While Epicharmus' *sisaron* and/or Hippocrates' *staphylinos* may be the parsnip, Dioscorides' *elaphoboscon* – an umbellifer with yellow flowers and a white, sweet and edible root – can only be this delectable root, and in a domesticated, cultivated form. The Romans were also aware of the parsnip – Pliny discusses it at length.

Whether the wild form was domesticated in Britain or the Romans brought a cultivated parsnip is not known. However, the parsnip appears in the *Læcboc of Bald* and the *Lacnunga*, both dating to the 10th century. The parsnip was an important starchy winter vegetable down the ages until it was superseded by the potato in the 18th century. In 1552 Tragus records the parsnip's extensive consumption, especially by the poor, and Gerard (1597) observes that 'The Parsneps nourish more than do the Turneps or the Carrots, and the nourishment is somewhat thicker, but not faultie nor bad … There is a good and pleasant foode or bread made of the rootes of Parsneps'. Parsnips are praised by many other authors too: for instance in 1683 Worlidge says they are 'in great use for a delicate sweet food' – the roots were often used to sweeten dishes in the absence of honey or sugar, expensive luxuries restricted to the wealthy – and in 1855 M'Intosh notes another use the parsnip was put to (quoted above).

Fortunately, a number of heritage varieties survive. A very hardy cultivar known by 1803, 'Hollow Crown' produces large, tasty roots. Considered at the time 'the best and most useful parsnip' and already 'improved' by 1852, the roots of 'Half Long Guernsey' are 'medium long, with a broad shoulder, gradually tapering downward. The white skin is smooth and attractive.' However, this description appeared before a (successful) scientific experiment was conducted between 1848 and 1850 by Professor James Buckman of the Royal Agricultural College in Cirencester. Desirous to discover whether a domesticated parsnip could be derived from the native species by selection, Buckman sowed seed of wild parsnip, selected the best roots, and then sowed the seed from these. He called the best root of the second generation 'The Student' and sent it to Messrs Suttons & Sons of Reading in 1850. Further improvement followed, as did many prizes, and this parsnip is still regarded as one of the finest. Perhaps selected from it, 'Tender and True' (1897), named after a popular song by Arthur Sullivan, is 'not quite so large … but more perfect in form, the quality is the very best, the skin is beautifully clear & smooth'.

OPPOSITE *Parsnip 'Tender and True', in the centre of the top row, among other root vegetables, including beetroots and turnips.*

Wee call them in English Vipers grasse, or Scorzonera …
The rootes hereof being preserved with sugar, as I have
done often, doe eat almost as delicate as the Eringus roote,
and no doubt is good to comfort and strengthen the
heart, and vitall spirits.

Gerard, 1597

SALSIFY & SCORZONERA
Tragopogon porrifolius & *Scorzonera hispanica*

Purple or common salsify, also known as the oyster plant because of its taste, is native to Mediterranean regions and is an overlooked vegetable. Although the young shoots may be eaten (the species name means 'leek-leaved'), salsify is primarily cultivated as a root vegetable. The roots, which look somewhat like a parsnip but do not reach the same girth, have white flesh and a mild, sweetish taste and are often simply boiled. If left to grow, this salsify has very attractive purple flowers, which close in the middle of the day, hence one of its common names as given by Gerard (1597) – 'Go to bed at noone'. Its other common name, goat's beard or goatsbeard, is a translation of the Greek genus name.

Salsify does not definitely appear in the medieval texts, although some commentators identify it as Albertus Magnus's *Oculus porce* or *flos campi*, which he describes as having a delectable root that is eaten. The first clear reference is by William Turner in 1548, who says 'Barba Hirci named in greeke Tragopogon … maye be called in englishe gotes bearde'. Turner, however, makes no mention of its cultivation as a vegetable, and neither does Daléchamp (1586), who does say it is planted in gardens. Gerard identifies salsify as *T. purpureus* or purple goatsbeard and says it was cultivated 'in gardens for the beautie of the flowers, almost every where', but does indicate also its cultivation as a vegetable, being of the opinion that the boiled, buttered root was of 'most pleasant meate and wholesome, in delicate taste farre surpassing either Parsnip or Carrot'. Parkinson (1629), who received his purple goatsbeard from Italy, dis-

cusses it together with the blue form. However, when enumerating their 'vertues' he also introduces the yellow goatsbeard, which is cultivated in the kitchen garden and is 'more fit for meate then medicine'. The yellow goatsbeard, or Western salsify, is *T. dubius*. Parkinson goes on to say that while the roots of the blue and purple are 'a little more bitter' they too are 'used as the yellow kind is'. Cultivation of salsify in the kitchen garden is noted by Ray in 1686, and M'Intosh (1855) reports that it has been 'hitherto confined to gardens of the first order, but would be worth the attention of amateurs, as affording an additional dish of vegetable diet'.

Another little-grown vegetable which has its keen supporters is scorzonera. Fairly similar in appearance to salsify, the long thin roots have white flesh but a black skin. Scorzonera is native to Spain and derives its name from the Catalonian *scurzon* meaning viper. Gerard calls it 'Vipers grasse' and says that in its native land the root was considered an antidote to the snake's bite. L'Obel (1576) reported that scorzonera was grown in French, Belgian and English gardens from Spanish seed, but according to M'Intosh its introduction from Spain to Britain occurred before 1526, adding that scorzonera was 'found in all our best gardens, but like salsify and skirret occupies one-fifth of the space that parsnips do'. Also like salsify, the roots are usually boiled, though Gerard mentions them preserved in sugar as a sweetmeat (see quote above).

OPPOSITE *Salsify (left) and scorzonera (right).*

TUBERS

Some rather exotic-looking tubers from North and South America can provide useful alternative winter vegetables. The Jerusalem artichoke has been known in Europe for centuries, while Oca de Peru and the tuberous nasturtium are relatively recent additions to the kitchen garden.

JERUSALEM ARTICHOKE

Helianthus tuberosus

Native to eastern North America, where it may have originated from the Ohio and Mississippi river valleys, the Jerusalem artichoke or sunchoke is a member of the sunflower genus and will produce similar cheerful yellow flowers. However, it is for its knobbly tubers that it is grown, which usefully can be dug up when required in the winter. Although rather fiddly and awkward to peel, they have a delicious nutty taste. Sir Walter Raleigh encountered Native Americans cultivating 'sunroots' in what is now Virginia in 1585, but the honour of introducing the plant to Europe belongs to the French explorer Samuel de Champlain, who found the Abenaki Indians cultivating the crop on Cape Cod in 1605.

The first person known to grow the Jerusalem artichoke in England was John Goodyer in 1617, who received two roots from Mr Franqueville of London; he was not impressed. In 1621 he wrote 'But in my judgment, which way soever they be drest and eaten they stir up and cause a filthie loathesome stinking winde with the bodie, thereby causing the belly to bee much pained and tormented.' The reason for this outcome is that unlike the potato which stores carbohydrate as starch, the Jerusalem artichoke does so as a polysaccharide called inulin, which is less digestible. However, some of the inulin is metabolized into fructose (rather than sucrose in the case of starch), making the Jerusalem artichoke a useful potato substitute for diabetics.

Of what he calls 'Potatoes of Canada' Parkinson (1629) says 'We in England, from some ignorant and idle head, have called them Artichokes of Jerusalem'. In fact the name is not as daft as Parkinson suggests: Jerusalem is a corruption of the Italian *girasole* for sunflower, meaning 'turning to the sun' (like sunflowers, the flowers follow the path of the sun), and the tubers do have a similar taste to globe artichoke hearts. The Jerusalem artichoke is very vigorous, which results in large harvests, though the plant may become invasive. And familiarity breeds contempt. Parkinson notes that even within a couple of decades of its introduction, the tuber had 'growne to be so common here with us at London, that even the most vulgar begin to despise them, whereas when they were first received among us, they were dainties for a Queene'.

The stigma of being a food for the poor lasted until the mid-19th century, when M'Intosh (1855) was able to state that its 'restoration to cultivation has commenced'. The Jerusalem artichoke received another boost during the Second World War, since unlike the potato it was not subject to rationing in Britain, and this much maligned vegetable continues to enjoy something of a deserved renaissance. Try them, but do bear in mind their rather anti-social side-effect.

OPPOSITE *Jerusalem artichokes.*

The [nasturtium] tubers should not be taken up for use before the latter end of autumn, after the early frosts, as they do not form until late in the season and are not affected by frost as long as they remain in the ground. When boiled like Carrots or Potatoes, the tubers are watery ... although the perfume is agreeable.

Vilmorin-Andrieux, 1885

TUBERS

TUBEROUS NASTURTIUM & OCA DE PERU

Tropaeolum tuberosum & *Oxalis tuberosa*

A couple of unusual and similar tubers, both native to South America and relatively recent additions to the vegetable garden, are the tuberous nasturtium (*Tropaeolum tuberosum*) and Oca de Peru (*Oxalis tuberosa*). The tuberous nasturtium is from the Andes, where it is known as *mashua* or *añu*, and is a very tough plant: it will produce a high yield on poor soils, at high altitudes and when smothered with weeds. The gorgeously speckled tubers have a somewhat peppery taste when eaten raw, which disappears when cooked. It was one of a number of exotic vegetables that the great French seed company Vilmorin-Andrieux imported and experimented with in the 19th century and detailed in their beautifully illustrated catalogue, translated into English as *The Vegetable Garden* (1885).

One word of caution to male readers, though, *mashua* is an anaphrodisiac. The Spanish chronicler and Jesuit Bernabe Cobo, who first travelled to South America in 1596 and stayed there for 61 years, recorded that the tuber was fed by Inca emperors to their armies 'that they should forget their wives', and in laboratory studies, male rats fed on *mashua* show a 45 per cent drop in testosterone levels.

Oca de Peru, oka or New Zealand yam (where it is said to have been introduced in 1869) was brought into cultivation in the central and southern Andes and remains an important staple. It is cultivated for its shoots and leaves, which can be eaten raw, and tubers, which if uncooked have a tangy flavour, but are more commonly boiled, resulting in a floury, potato texture and taste. Oca was introduced into Europe in 1830 and is another exotic grown by Vilmorin-Andrieux, whose catalogue compared its looks to the potato 'Vitelotte' (see p. 34) and described how in South America, in order to rid the tubers of their acidity, they were put 'into woollen bags and [exposed] to the action of the sun, the effect of which is that in a few days they become floury and sweet'. Also according to the catalogue, two varieties had been introduced into France, 'the Yellow and the Red'.

OPPOSITE *Tuberous nasturtium (above) and Oca de Peru (below).*

CHRONOLOGY of introduction of fruits and vegetables to Britain

INDIGENOUS FRUITS	ROMAN FRUIT INTRODUCTIONS	DARK AGES & MEDIEVAL FRUIT INTRODUCTIONS	TUDOR FRUIT INTRODUCTIONS	LATER FRUIT INTRODUCTIONS
Blackberry	Almond	Bitter orange	Apricot	Garden strawberry
Bullace	Apple	Citron	Blackcurrant	(18th century)
Gooseberry	Black mulberry	Filbert	Redcurrant	Green gage (18th century)
Hazel nut	Damson	Lemon	Sweet orange	Mexican lime (17th century)
Red raspberry	Fig	Medlar	Whitecurrant	Mirabelle (16th century)
Sweet cherry	Peach	Melon		Nectarine (17th century)
(gean or mazzard)	Pear	Quince		Pineapple (17th century)
Wood strawberry	Plum			Rhubarb (18th century)
	Sour cherry			
	Sweet chestnut			
	Vine			
	Walnut			

INDIGENOUS VEGETABLES	ROMAN VEGETABLE INTRODUCTIONS	DARK AGES & MEDIEVAL VEGETABLE INTRODUCTIONS	TUDOR VEGETABLE INTRODUCTIONS	LATER VEGETABLE INTRODUCTIONS
Asparagus, wild	Asparagus	Alexanders	Aubergine	Broccoli (18th century)
Broad bean (6th century BC)	Cabbage	Celery	Bean, green (pole and dwarf)	Brussels sprout (19th century)
Cabbage, wild	Carrot	Kale	Beetroot	Cardoon (17th century)
Carrot, wild	Cucumber	Radish	Cauliflower	Celeriac (18th century)
Celery, wild	Garlic (probably)	Shallot	Chard	Courgette (20th century)
Chickweed	Leek	Spinach	Chilli and sweet pepper	Florence fennel (18th century)
Chicory	Lettuce		Globe artichoke	Jerusalem artichoke
Kale	Onion (probably)		Kohlrabi	(17th century)
Parsnip, wild	Turnip		Marrow	Oca de Peru
Pea (6th century BC)			Potato	Pea, garden (17th century)
Radish, wild			Pumpkin & squash	Purslane (17th century)
Sea kale			Salsify	Scarlet runner bean
			Scorzonera	(17th century)
			Tomato	Tuberous nasturtium
			Sweet corn	

USEFUL ADDRESSES Organizations, Suppliers and Gardens to Visit

ORGANIZATIONS

Royal Horticultural Society
www.rhs.org.uk

Heritage Seed Library, Garden Organic
www.gardenorganic.org.uk/hsl

Common Ground
www.commonground.org.uk

East of England Apples and Orchards Project
www.applesandorchards.org.uk

National Fruit Collection
www.nationalfruitcollection.org.uk

Orange Pippin
www.orangepippin.com

Seed Savers Exchange
www.seedsavers.org

UK FRUIT AND SEED SUPPLIERS

Agroforestry Research Trust
46 Hunters Moon, Dartington,
Totnes, TQ9 6JT
www.agroforestry.co.uk

Alan Romans
72, North St, Kettlebridge, Fife, KY15 7QJ
www.alanromans.com

Brogdale Farm,
Brogdale Road, Faversham, Kent, ME13 8XZ
www.brogdalecollections.co.uk

Chiltern Seeds,
Bortree Stile, Ulverston, Cumbria, LA12 7PB
www.chilternseeds.co.uk

Dundry Nurseries
Bamfurlong Lane, Cheltenham, GL51 6SL
www.dundrynurseries.co.uk/plist.asp

Keepers Nursery,
East Farleigh, Maidstone, Kent, ME15 0LE
www.keepers-nursery.co.uk

Real Seeds,
PO Box 18, Newport near Fishguard,
Pembrokeshire, SA65 0AA
www.realseeds.co.uk

R.V. Roger Ltd,
The Nurseries, Malton Road, Pickering,
North Yorkshire, YO18 7JW
http://rvroger.co.uk

Suffolk Herbs
Monks Farm, Coggeshall Road, Kelvedon,
Essex, CO5 9PG
www.suffolkherbs.com

Thomas Etty Esq.
Seedsman's Cottage, Puddlebridge, Ilminster,
Somerset, TA19 9RL
www.thomasetty.co.uk

Victoriana Nursery Gardens,
Challock, Nr Ashford, Kent, TN25 4DG
www.victoriananursery.co.uk

GARDENS TO VISIT

The following gardens have working vegetable
gardens and orchards where primarily heritage
varieties are cultivated

Audley End Organic Kitchen Garden
(English Heritage)
Off London Road, Saffron Walden,
Essex, CB11 4JF

Brogdale Farm, home of the National Fruit
Collection – address given above

Garden Organic
Ryton Gardens, Nr. Coventry, Warwickshire,
CV8 3LG
www.gardenorganic.org.uk/hsl

The Lost Gardens of Heligan,
Pentewan, St Austell, Cornwall PL26 6EN
www.heligan.com

West Dean Gardens
West Dean, Nr Chichester, West Sussex
PO18 0RX
www.westdean.org.uk/Garden/Home.aspx

US FRUIT AND SEED SUPPLIERS

Amishland Heirloom Seeds
Box 365, Reamstown, PA 17567-0365
lisa@amishlandseeds.com

Burpee Seeds and Plants
300 Park Avenue, Warminster, PA 18974
www.burpee.com

Eden Brothers
PO Box 1115, Dahlonega, GA 30533
www.edenbrothers.com/store

Fedco Seeds,
PO Box 520, Waterville, ME 04903
www.fedcoseeds.com

Granny's Heirloom Seeds
PO Box 284, Bolivar, MO 65613
www.grannysheirloomseeds.com

GRDN
103 Hoyt St., Brooklyn, NY 11217
info@grdnbklyn.com

Hancock Shaker Village
PO Box 927, Pittsfield, MA 01202

Heirloom Seeds
http://www.heirloomseeds.com

Homeland Preparedness
PO Box 997, Mars Hill, NC 28754
service@homelandpreparedness.com

Native Seeds
3584 E. River Road, Tucson, AZ 85718
www.nativeseeds.org

Organica Seed
PO Box 611, Wilbraham, MA 01095
www.organicaseed.com

Rose Red & Lavender
653 Metropolitan Ave, Brooklyn, NY 11211
lavender@roseredandlavender.com

Seeds Now
PO Box 1820, Thousand Oaks, CA 91358
support@seedsnow.com

Seeds of Change
PO Box 4908, Rancho Dominguez, CA 90220
www.seedsofchange.com

Thomas Jefferson's Monticello
Thomas Jefferson Foundation
PO Box 316, Charlottesville, VA 22902
info@monticello.org
www.monticello.org

Trees of Antiquity
20 Wellsona Road, Paso Robles, CA 93446
www.treesofantiquity.com

Victory Seed Company
PO Box 192, Molalla, OR 97038
www.victoryseeds.com

No one studying the subject of the history of fruits can fail to acknowledge the contribution of Frederick Roach, whose masterful and comprehensive *Cultivated Fruits of Britain* was published in 1985. Of an older vintage but no less significant to the study of vegetables is 'History of Garden Vegetables', a series of articles by E. Lewis Sturtevant printed in *The American Naturalist* (1887–91) and subsequently published as *Sturtevant's Notes on Edible Plants* (ed. U. P. Hedrick, 1919). Other resources that have proved invaluable are *Domestication of Plants in the Old World* by Daniel Zohary and Maria Hopf (3rd ed., 2000), John Harvey's *Mediaeval Gardens* (1981) and *British Botanical and Horticultural Literature before 1800* by Blanche Henrey (1975). For those who wish to know more about kitchen gardening, Susan Campbell's *Charleston Kedding: A History of Kitchen Gardening* (1996) is an insightful and entertaining read.

Other books include Jonathan Roberts' *Cabbages and Kings* (2001) and Christopher Stocks' *Forgotten Fruits* (2008).

The quote on p. 12 is from 'New Plant Foods in Roman Britain – Dispersal and Social Access' by M. van der Veen, A. Livarda and A. Hill (2008), in *Environmental Archaeology* 13:1, 11–36, p. 11. The paper on the identification of carrots and parsnips in ancient sources referred to is: John Stolarczyk & Jules Janick (2011), 'Carrot: History and Iconography', in *Chronica Horticulturae*, 51:2, 13–18; and for early Chinese literary references to the aubergine, see Jin-Xiu Wang, Tian-Gang Gao and Sandra Knapp (2008), 'Ancient Chinese Literature Reveals Pathways of Eggplant Domestication', *Annals of Botany* 102: 891–7.

Primary sources are essential when researching a book such as this, but they also pose a problem of access. Thankfully, today's horticultural and garden historian has a wonderful resource in the Biodiversity Heritage Library (www.biodiversitylibrary.org), which holds a catalogue of literally thousands of early and rare monographs and periodicals, all of which may be downloaded at no cost. The main ones used in writing this book are as follows, in chronological order:

Herodotus (*c.* 430 BC), *The Histories.*

Theophrastus (3rd century BC), *Historia Plantarum; De Causis Plantarum.*

Cato the Elder (*c.* 160 BC), *De Agri Cultura.*

Varro (1st century BC), *Rerum rusticarum libri III.*

Columella (mid-1st century BC), *De re rustica.*

Pliny the Elder (*c.* AD 77–79), *Naturalis Historia.*

Palladius (4th century AD), *Opus agriculturae.*

Apicius (late 4th or early 5th century AD), *De Re Coquinaria.*

Dioscorides (late 1st century AD), *De Materia Medica.*

Benedict of Aniane (*c.* 794–812), *Capitulare de Villis.*

Bald (*c.* 925–40), *Læcboc of Bald.*

British Library MS. Harley 585 (*c.* 1000), *Lacnunga.*

Ælfric of Eynsham (*c.* 995), *Glossary.*

Hildegard of Bingen, abbess (1150), *Liber Simplicis Medicinae* (later called *Physica*).

Ibn Bassal (*c.* 1080), *Diwan al-Filaha* (Book of Agriculture).

Neckam, A. (*c.* 1180), *De Naturis Rerum; (c.* 1213), *De Laudibus Divinae Sapientiae.*

Ibn-al-'Awwam (late 12th century), *Kitab al-Filahah* (The Book of Agriculture).

Albertus Magnus (*c.* 1260), *De Vegetabilis et Plantis.*

Crescentiis, Petrus de (1305), *Liber ruralium commodorum.*

Gardener, J. (*c.* 1400), *The Feate of gardening.*

Mayer MS (*c.* 1450).

Treveris, P. (1526), *Grete Herball.*

Ruellius, J. (1536), *De natura stirpium libri tres.*

Fuchs, L. (1542), *De Historia Stirpium.*

Mattioli, P. A. G. (Matthiolus) (1548 and 1554), *Commentarii, in Sex Libros Pedacii Dioscorides.*

Tragus, H. (J. Bock) (1552), *De Stirpium,* etc.

Turner, W. (1548), *The Names of Herbes; (1551), Nieuwe Herball.*

Clusius, C. (1557), *Histoire des plantes.*

Tusser, T. (1573), *Five hundred pointes of good husbandrie.*

de L'Obel, M. (1576), *Stirpium Observationes; (1570), Stirpium Adversaria Nova* (with P. Pena)

Lyte, H. (1578), *A Niewe Herball, or Historie of Plantes.*

Dodoens, R. (1583), *Stirpium historiae pemptades sex.*

Daléchamps, J. (1586), *Historia generalis plantarum.*

Alpinus (Alpini, P.) (1591), *De Plantis Aegypti.*

Gerard, J. (1597), *The Herball or generall historie of plantes; (1599), Catalogus arborum, fruticum ac plantarum tam indigenarum quam exoticarum in horto Johannis Gerardi … nascentium.* Repr. by Jackson, B. D. (1876), *A catalogue of plants cultivated in the garden of John Gerard, in the years 1596–1599.*

Parkinson, J. (1629), *Paradisi in Sole Paradisus Terrestris.*

Gerard, J., ed. Johnson, T. (1636), *The Herbal.*

Rea, J. (1655), *Flora;* expanded ed. (1676), *Flora, Ceres, et Pomona.*

Meager, L. (1670; 2nd ed. 1683), *The English Gardener.*

Worlidge, J. (2nd ed., 1683), *Systema Horti-culturae.*

Rauwolf, L., trans. Ray, J. (1693), *Dr. Leonhart Rauwolf's Travels into the Eastern Countries.*

Ray, J. (3 vols, 1686–1704), *Historia Plantarum.*

de la Quintinye, J.-B. *Le parfait jardinier,* trans. Evelyn, J. (1693), *The Compleat Gard'ner.*

Bauhin, J. (1651), *Historia plantarum universalis.*

Evelyn, J. (1699), *Acetaria. A discourse of sallets.*

Townsend, B. (1726), *The Complete Seedsman.*

Langley, B. (1728), *New Principles of Gardening; (1729), Pomona: or, the Fruit Garden Illustrated.*

Switzer, S. (1728), *A Compendious Method for the Raising of,* etc.

Miller, P. (1731), *The Gardeners Dictionary.*

de la Chesnaye, F.-A. (1751), *Dictionnaire universel d'agriculture et de jardinage.*

Wheeler, J. (1758), *Botanist's and Gardener's Dictionary.*

Stevenson, H. (7th ed., 1766), *The gentleman gard'ner instructed,* etc.

Mawe, T. & Abercrombie, J. (1767), *Every Man his own Gardener.*

Gibson, J. (1768), *The Fruit-Gardener.*

Mawe, T. (1779), *The British Fruit-Gardener; and Art of Pruning.*

Tollard, C. (1805), *Traité des végétaux.*

Brookshaw, G. (1812), *Pomona Britannica.*

Phillips, H. (1822), *History of Cultivated Vegetables.*

Loudon, J. C. (3rd ed. 1825), *An Encyclopaedia of Gardening; (1830), Hortus Britannicus.*

Lindley, G., ed. Lindley, J. (1831), *A Guide to the Orchard and Fruit Garden.*

Vilmorin, A. et cie. (1850), *Le Jardin Potager;* trans. (1885), *The Vegetable Garden; (1856), Description des Plantes potagères; (1883), Les Plantes potagères.*

M'Intosh, C. (vol. I, 1853, vol. II, 1855), *The Book of the Garden.*

Hogg, R. (5th ed., 1884), *The Fruit Manual.*

Henslow, G. (1912), *The Origin and History of our Garden Vegetables.*

INDEX

Numbers in **bold** refer to the main discussion of a fruit or vegetable

Abenaki 217
Abercrombie, John 21
Adam and Eve 68, 126
Ælfric 15, 42, 76, 98, 132, 135, 136, 143
Afghanistan 94, 106, 126, 190
Africa 16, 61, 136; North 24, 30, 49, 50, 84, 105, 116, 166; south 190
al-'Awwam, Ibn 119
Alberti, Leonardo 50
Aleppo 27, 30
Alexandria 116, 166, 189
Alexanders **116–17**
Alexander the Great 41, 64, 140, 143
alliums 76–83; see individual types
almond 41, **136–37**, 143
Alpinus, Prosper (Prospero Alpini) 27, 30, 112
America: Central 90, 177; North 24, 67, 71, 101, 120, 132, 143, 165, 178, 217; South 16, 21, 33, 119, 120, 132, 170, 193, 218
Americans, Native 170, 178, 217
Andalusia 119
Andes 33, 89, 120, 177, 218
Anne of Denmark, Queen 19, 33
aphrodisiac qualities 41, 83, 105, 115, 120
Aphrodite 126, 165
Apicius 24, 30, 75, 93, 94, 106, 136, 140, 144, 169, 190, 194
apple 12, 14, 15, 16, 41, **126–31**, 165, 181; crab 12, 126
apricot 16, **40–41**, 136
Arabs 49, 50, 55, 105, 174
Archilochus 68
Aristotle 83, 169
Armenia 41, 159, 186, 190
artichoke: globe **104–05**; Jerusalem 18, **216–17**
Ashkelon 80
Ashworth, Fred 178
Asia 16, 24, 46, 49, 53, 55, 57, 58, 64, 93, 111, 144, 166; Central 76, 83, 119; Minor 140, 162; southwest 84, 119, 189; western 139, 181, 210
asparagus 21, **24–25**, 27, 105
Assyria 45, 135
Athenaeus 94
aubergine 18, 33, **174–75**
Austen, Jane 41
Australia 54, 119

Bald's Leechbook, see Læcboc of Bald
Balkans 139, 140, 143
Banks, Sir Joseph 53, 119, 198
Bao, Wang 174
Barbados 54, 193
Barnes, James 98, 193
Bassal, Ibn 27, 174
Bauhin, Johann 102, 166
bean: broad 21, **84–87**, 106; French 16, **88–89**; scarlet runner 16, 89, **90–91**
beans 21, 84–91, 101, 178, 181; see individual types
Becket, Thomas 68, 71
Beddington Park 16, 50
Bede, Venerable 189
beet 12; leaf 93, 169; sea 12, 93, 169; see also chard
beetroot **92–93**, 169
Belgium 57, 197, 207
Benedict of Aniane 14
Benzoni, Girolamo 27
Bible 33, 41, 76, 186
Bicton 98
blackberry 12, 41, **132–33**; American 72, 132
blackcurrant 57, **58–59**
Black Death, the 16, 67, 189
Black Sea 45, 186
blackthorn see sloe
Blenheim Palace 190

Bliss, George 21
Bobart, Jacob the Elder 54
Bock, Jerome see Tragus, Hieronymus
Bolivia 36
Bouschet, Henri 189
brassicas 27, 181, **194–203**; see individual types
Brazil 54, 177, 193
Britain 16, 21, 27, 30, 33, 41, 61, 71, 75, 93, 115, 116, 119, 139, 143, 156, 166, 169, 197, 213; Bronze Age 72, 150; Iron Age 84, 106, 150; Neolithic 132; Roman 12, 14, 24, 42, 45, 67, 68, 94, 98, 126, 136, 144, 181, 198, 210, 213
Brittany 75, 76, 105
broccoli 27, 30, **194–95**
Brompton Park Nursery 41
Bronze Age 42, 136
Brown, Lancelot 'Capability' 189
Brussels sprout 30, **196–97**
Buckman, Professor James 213
bullace see plum, bullace
Burghley, Lord see Cecil, Sir William
Burma 46

cabbage 30, 181, **198–201**; wild 12, 30, 202
Cadfan, Cadwallon ap 210
calabrese see broccoli
California 50, 53, 54, 72, 115
Callejon de Huaylas 89
Canary Islands 33
Canterbury 71, 126; Archbishop of 68, 98
Capitulare de Villis 14, 30, 80, 94, 111, 150, 165, 202
capsicums 176–77
cardoon **105**
Carew, Sir Francis 16, 42, 50
carrot **94–97**, 166, 213; wild 12, 94
Carthage 53
Caspian Sea 45, 135
Cato 14, 24, 135, 144, 189, 202
Caucasus 71, 150, 186, 190
cauliflower 24, **26–29**, 30, 194
Caus, Salomon de 19
Cayenne 193
Cecil, Sir William 16; Sir Robert, 1st Earl of Salisbury 19, 58, 105
celeriac **166–67**
celery **166–67**; wild 12
Champlain, Samuel de 217
Chanca, Diego Álvarez 177
chard 93, **168–69**
Charlemagne 14, 30, 94, 116, 165, 181, 202
Charles II 193
Charles VIII, king of France 147
Chaucer 136, 150
Chengda, Fan 53
cherry 16, 19, 41, **42–45**, 57, 132, 136, 165; acid or sour **44–45**; sweet 12, **42–43**; wild 12
chestnut, sweet **140–41**
chicory **206–09**
chilli 16, 18, 33, **176–77**; see also pepper, sweet
China 16, 19, 41, 46, 49, 50, 64, 71, 98, 111, 112, 119, 126, 143
Chiswick 61, 67, 68, 71, 132
cider 16, 129
Circe 83
citron **46–47**, 53, 54
citrus 46–55; see individual types
Claude, Duchess of Brittany 159
Cleopatra 189
Clusius, Carolus (Charles de l'Écluse) 18, 27, 33
Cobbett, William 178
cob nut **138–39**; see also filbert, hazelnut
Cobo, Bernabe 218
Coe, Jervaise 153
Colnbrook 129
Columbus, Christopher 16, 53, 89, 101, 120, 170, 177, 193

Columella 14, 64, 111, 116, 136, 150, 169, 198
Connover, S. B. 24
Conquistadors 16, 33, 89
Cook, James 33, 53, 198
Corfu 46
Corsica 140
Cortés, Hernan 120
Cotán, Juan Sanchéz 105
courgette **100–01**, 170; see also marrow
Crescentiis (Petrus de Crescentiis) 119
Crete 68, 136, 165
Cromwell, Oliver 193
Crump, Thomas 190
Crusaders/Crusades 15, 49, 71, 80, 119, 156
cucumber 12, 21, 76, **98–99**, 170, 190
Cucurbitaceae 98, 115, 170
cucurbits 98–101; see individual types
currants **56–59**; see individual types
Cyprus 27

Daléchamps, Jacques 27, 194, 197, 214
Damascus 150, 156
damson see plum, damson
Danckerts, Hendrick 193
Dark Ages 54, 68, 132, 139, 190
Darwin, Charles 61
Dawnay, Marmaduke 27
Demeter 68
Denmark 42, 132
Dionysos 68, 102, 186
Dioscorides 24, 64, 94, 97, 112, 116, 169, 190, 198, 213
Dodoens, Rembert (Rembertus Dodonaeus) 18, 207
Domesday Book 144, 189
drupe 41, 143, 150
drupelet 72, 132
Dumas, Alexandre 76
Durham Account Rolls 143

East Malling Research Station 72
Eden, Garden in 33, 41, 83, 126
Edinburgh 112
Edward I 15, 61, 67, 165
egg-plant see aubergine
Egypt 27, 30, 49; ancient 12, 68, 71, 76, 83, 98, 106, 111, 115, 174, 186, 190, 210
Egyptians 12, 24, 46
Eleanor of Castile, Queen 15, 49, 126, 165
Eleanor of Castile (wife of Charles III) 49
Eleusinian Mysteries 84
Elizabeth I 16, 19, 33, 42, 49, 94, 106
Ely 42, 189
England 15, 16, 18, 19, 24, 30, 33, 53, 54, 105, 111, 112, 120, 190
Engler, Adolf 46
Epicharmus 94, 213
Epic of Gilgamesh 98, 186, 190
Evelyn, John 76, 115, 166, 177, 193, 198
Exodus 76

Fenn, Robert 36
fennel: Florence **102–03**; giant 102
fig 12, 64, **68–69**
filbert **138–39**; see also cob nut, hazelnut
First World War 21, 120
Flanders 19, 45, 61, 182
Florida 53, 54
Fontainebleau 49
forcing 21, 24, 36, 64, 97, 98, 112, 202, 207
Forme of Cury, The 119
France 19, 45, 57, 72, 75, 76, 80, 94, 106, 111, 115, 119, 126, 144, 147, 170, 181, 190, 207
Frézier, Amédée-François 75
Frogmore 42, 75
Fuchs, Leonhart 57, 89, 93
Fulham Nursery 68

gage see plum, gage
Gage, Sir William 159
Gardener, Jon 119
Garden of the Hesperides 126, 165
Garden Organic 11
garlic 12, 76, 80, **82–83**, 111, 210; wild 83
Genesis 12, 68, 126, 136, 186
genetics 106
Gerard, John 18, 19, 27, 30, 33, 50, 57, 58, 61, 67, 71, 76, 83, 89, 90, 93, 94, 105, 111, 116, 132, 135, 136, 139, 143, 144, 150, 165, 169, 170, 174, 177, 181, 190, 198, 202, 210, 213, 214
Gerard of Wales 71
Germany 30, 93, 94, 120, 174, 207
Gibson, John 42, 45
glasshouses 16, 21, 24, 67, 97, 98, 186, 189, 190, 193
Glastonbury 106
Glossary see Ælfric
Goodyer, John 217
Googe, Barnaby 89
gooseberry 16, 57, **60–63**
grafting 12, 143, 165
grape 14, 19, 21, **186–89**; see also vine, vineyard, wine
grapefruit 54
Greece 54, 68, 83, 94, 135, 136, 140, 143, 159, 166, 186
Greeks 45, 68, 72, 94, 102, 105, 106, 111, 116, 126, 136, 143, 144, 165, 169, 207, 210
greenhouses 21, 207; see also glasshouses
Grubb, Norman H. 72
Guilá Naquitz 101, 178
Gwyn, Nell 50

Haiti 27
Hampton Court palace 21, 75, 189, 193
Hanmer, Sir Thomas 147
Haraldskær Woman 132
Harris, Richard 16, 45
Harvey, John 16
Hatfield House 19, 58, 105, 153
Hathor 186
Hawkins, John 33
hazelnut 12, 139; see also cob nut, filbert
head gardeners 12, 21, 186, 193
Hecate 83
Heligan, Lost Gardens of 193
Henry II King of France 105
Henry III 16, 71, 72, 144
Henry IV 144
Henry VI 49
Henry VIII 16, 41, 45, 61, 67, 75, 105, 129, 135, 150
Henslow, George 119, 202
Hera 126
herbals 18
Hercules 126
Heritage Seed Library 84
Hermes 83
Herodotus 76, 111, 115
Hildegard of Bingen, St 75
Himalaya 76, 98, 143
Hippocrates 94, 115, 213
Hitt, Thomas 189
Hogg, Robert 21, 75, 129, 135, 139, 143, 144, 147, 165
Holinshed, Ralph 170; Chronicles 143
Holland 19, 21, 57, 93, 97, 106, 182, 193
Homer 12, 84, 144, 166, 186
hotbed 21, 24, 98, 190
hothouse see glasshouses

Iliad, The 84
Inca 218
India 16, 46, 49, 50, 55, 64, 98, 106, 112, 174, 193
Indus 136
Ingram, Thomas 42, 75
Ireland 11, 33, 36
Iroquois 178
Israel/Israelites 12, 76, 186, 190

Italy 30, 33, 46, 101, 115, 120, 150, 159, 177, 194, 197, 210, 214

James I 19, 27, 71
Janick, Jules 94
Japan 111, 170
Jefferson, Thomas 36, 102, 202
Jesus 186
John, King 16, 64, 140
Johnson, Thomas 90
Jordan 12, 68, 106
Judgment of Paris 126, 165

kale 30, **202–03**; sea 12, 202
Keens, Michael 75
King's Langley 15, 126
Knight, Thomas Andrew 42, 57, 153
Knights Templar 71
kohlrabi 27, **30–31**
Kos 115
Kyrgyzstan 126, 143

Lacnunga 14, 24, 64, 75, 84, 111, 126, 132, 181, 198, 210, 213
Læcboc of Bald 14, 64, 71, 75, 76, 84, 98, 111, 126, 132, 135, 144, 150, 181, 190, 198, 210, 213
Lambeth Palace 68, 98, 210
Langley, Batty 80, 162
Laxton, Thomas 75, 90
Laxton Brothers nursery 58, 153
leek 12, 14, 76, 80, **210–11**
lemon **52–53**
lettuce 12, 14, **114–15**; prickly 115
lime **54–55**
Lindley, George 61; John 61, 136, 147, 159
Linear B 166
Linneus, Carl 120
Little Ice Age 143, 189
L'Obel, Matthias de 93, 198, 214
loganberry 72, 132
London 24, 27, 36, 106, 190, 193, 210
Loudon, John Claudius 30, 68, 98, 132, 165, 174, 194, 197
Louis XIV 24, 27
Louis XVI 36
Lydgate, John 49, 53
Lyte, Henry 18, 27, 93, 111, 120, 156, 174

M'Intosh, Charles 33, 105, 106, 116, 135, 147, 165, 166, 169, 170, 174, 181, 182, 190, 193, 194, 198, 213, 214, 217
Magnus, Albertus 15, 46, 49, 61, 94, 111, 169, 174, 181, 190, 198, 214
Mainz *Herbarius* 57
maize 101, 178; *see also* sweet corn
Manichaeism 190
Marie Antoinette 36
marrow **100–01**, 170; *see also* courgette
Martyr, Peter 177
Mary, Queen of Scots 33
Mary II, Queen 21, 193
Matthiolus (Mattioli, Pietro Andrea Gregorio) 30, 57, 93, 94, 105, 120
Mawe, Thomas 21, 27, 67, 72, 84, 112, 136, 139, 156, 165, 166, 174, 181, 190
Mayer manuscript 80
Meager, Leonard 24, 41, 106
Medici, Catherine de 105
medicinal qualities 14, 15, 53, 58, 72, 83, 94, 102, 112, 115, 136
Medieval Warm Period 49, 67, 189
medlar 19, **134–35**, 150
Meech, Rev. W. W. 165
melon 12, 21, 76, 170, 186; cantaloupe 190; honeydew 190; muskmelon **190–91**
Mendel, Gregor 106

Mesopotamia 71, 76, 165, 186, 210
Metz 162
Mexico 54, 89, 90, 101, 120, 170, 178
Michaud, Joseph François 80
Miller, Philip 27, 84, 90, 102, 105, 135, 159, 169, 174, 194
Min 115
mirabelle *see* plum, mirabelle
monasteries 14, 126, 189
Monticello 36, 202
Moors 119, 120
Moses 46
mulberry: black 14, 21, **70–71**; red 71; white 19, 71
muskmelon **190–91**; *see also* melon

Nancy 162
Naples 147, 174
nasturtium, tuberous **218–19**
National Fruit Collection (NFC) 11, 41, 61, 126
Neckam, Alexander 15, 49, 53, 64, 84, 135, 136, 165, 190, 207
nectarine **64–67**, 136
Neolithic 12, 68, 75, 106
Nero, emperor 210
New Guinea 106
New Zealand 119; spinach 119; yam 218
Newton, Sir Isaac 129
nightshade, deadly 33, 120
Noah 186
Norse mythology 126
Norton, Dr J. B. 24
nuts 136–43; *see individual types*

Oaxaca 100, 120, 178
Oca de Peru **218–19**
Odyssey, The 12, 126, 144, 166, 186
Odysseus 83, 126
Old Testament 12, 71, 136
olive 12
onion 12, **76–79**, 111, 210
orange **48–51**, 53; bitter 16, **50–51**; mandarin 50; sweet **48–49**, 50
orangerie 19, 49
Ovid 75, 132
Oxford Physic Garden 54

Padua Botanic Garden 112
Palestine 49, 50, 55, 80
Palladius 14, 169
Paludanus, Bernhard 193
Paris 36, 76
Parkinson, John 27, 42, 46, 53, 58, 61, 67, 72, 84, 89, 93, 105, 116, 129, 135, 136, 143, 144, 150, 153, 156, 165, 174, 189, 214, 217
Parmentier, Antoine Augustine 36
parsnip 94, 181, **212–13**; wild 12, 213
Passover 68
pea 21, **106–09**; mangetout 106; petit pois 106; snap 106; snow 106; wild 106
pea, asparagus 106
peach 16, 41, **64–67**, 136, 165
pear 12, 15, 16, 41, 126, **144–49**, 181
pepper, sweet 16, 33, **176–77**
Pepys, Samuel 50, 98
Persia 41, 49, 55, 64, 115, 119, 135, 136, 190
Peru 33, 36, 89, 120, 170, 218
pineapple 21, **192–93**
pinkcurrant 56–57
Pleistocene 136
Pliny the Elder 14, 24, 30, 41, 42, 45, 64, 68, 75, 76, 83, 84, 94, 98, 105, 111, 115, 115, 126, 132, 135, 136, 139, 144, 150, 144, 150, 165, 169, 181, 189, 190, 194, 198, 202, 210, 213
plum 41, 136, **150–63**; bullace 12, **156–57**; damson **156–57**; gage **158–59**; mirabelle **162–63**
Plutarch 165

Polo, Marco 190
pome 126, 165
pomegranate 12
pomelo 50, 54
Pomona 12
Portugal 169
potato 11, 16, 18, 21, **32–37**, 89, 120, 174, 181
potato, sweet 18, 33
Potato Famine, Irish 11, 36
Potter, Beatrix 115
Priapus 12
Prometheus 102
pumpkin 16, 101, **170–73**; *see also* squash
pyramids 76, 111
Pythagorus 84

Quesada, Gonzalo Jiminez de 33
quince 16, 19, 41, 126, **164–65**
Quintinye, Jean-Bapstiste de la 147

radicchio *see* chicory
radish 12, 76, **110–11**, 181; wild 111
Raleigh, Sir Walter 16, 33, 217
raspberry 12, 41, 71, **72–73**, 75
Rauwolf, Leonhard 27, 30
Ray, John 169, 207, 214
Rea, John 61, 67, 135
redcurrant **56–57**
rhubarb **112–13**
Ribston 71
Rivers: Thomas 41, 67, 153; Nursery 41, 153
Robenhausen 94
Roger the gardener 98
Romans 12–13, 30, 41, 46, 49, 50, 53, 67, 68, 72, 76, 82, 94, 106, 111, 115, 116, 136, 140, 143, 144, 165, 186, 202, 207, 210, 213
Rome 53, 68, 84
Rosaceae 41
Royal Horticultural Society (RHS) 11, 42, 67, 68, 71, 72, 129, 132, 139, 153
Ruellius, Johannes 57, 105, 106, 116, 198
Russia 112
rutabaga 30, 182

salad 21, 111, **115–17**, 207; *see individual types*
salsify **214–15**
Sanskrit 50, 174
Sappho 181
Saracens 46, 119
Sargon II, King 45
Sasanians 119
scorzonera **214–15**
scallion (Welsh onion) 76, 80
Scotland 33, 126, 129, 182, 202
scurvy 54
Seed Savers Exchange 11
Seilenos (Silenus) 186
Shakespeare, William 49, 144, 170, 189
shallot 76, **80–81**
Shifriss, Oved 101
Sicily 49, 50, 53, 119, 169, 194
silk industry 19, 21, 71
Silk Road 41, 64
Sina, Ibn 174
sloe 12, 150
Solanaceae 16, 33, 120, 174–77
Solomon, King 41
Somerset House 19
Spain 27, 49, 50, 76, 119, 174, 177, 214
spinach **118–19**
squash 101, **170–73**, 178; *see also* pumpkin
Stephenson, George 98
Stevenson, Henry 102
Stolarczyk, John 94
stoves 21

strawberry 41, **74–75**, 132; wood 12, 75
Sukkot 46
Sutton's seeds (Suttons) 21, 30, 76, 84, 197, 213
Sweden 182
sweet corn 11, 18, **178–79**; *see also* maize
Swift, Jonathan 98
Switzer, Stephen 102, 166, 194
Syria 27, 49, 106, 156

Tahiti 54
Taíno 33, 178
Talmud 83
Tasmania 119
Tehuacan Valley 89, 170
Telende, Henry 193
Tenochtítlan 120
Teynham 16
Thailand 54, 98
Theobalds 16, 18, 19
Theophrastus 12, 24, 46, 64, 111, 116, 132, 135, 143, 150, 169, 198, 202
'Three Sisters, The' 178
Tiberius, emperor 98
Tibet 112
tobacco 16, 33
Toledo 27, 174
Tollard, Claude 174
tomato 16, 18, 21, 33, 89, **120–23**, 174
Torah 46
Tower of London 15, 61, 67, 165
Townsend, Benjamin 90, 210
Townshend, Charles 'Turnip' 181–82
Tradescant, John, the Elder 19, 57, 58, 105, 147, 150; the Younger 71
Tragus, Hieronymus 89, 170, 174, 213
Treveris, Peter 150
Turkey 72, 106, 112, 139
Turner, William 24, 41, 46, 57, 61, 72, 89, 94, 98, 105, 111, 132, 135, 136, 143, 156, 181, 207, 214
turnip 14, 30, **180–83**; wild 181
Tusser, Thomas 18, 42, 67, 75, 139, 156, 165
Tutankhamun 76, 136, 166
Twelfth Night 84

Ur 76, 98

Varro 14, 144
Veitch Nursery 72, 106, 182
Venus 75
Versailles 49
Vertumnus 12
Vilmorin 76, 97, 106, 218
vine 12, 16, 186–89; *see also* grape, vineyard, wine
vineyard 12, 42, 94, 186, 189; *see also* grape, vine, wine
Virginia 217
Virú Valley 170
Volga 112
Vries, Hugo de 106

walnut 14, **142–43**; black 143
Wardon Abbey 144
watermelon 190
Westminster 144; Abbey 84, 135, 150; Palace of 15
Wheeler, James 166
whitecurrant **56–57**
Wight, Isle of 83
Windebank, Sir Thomas 16
wine 12, 186, 189; *see also* grape, vine, vineyard
Wolf, John 16, 41
Wolfskill, William 50
Wolsey, Cardinal 75
Worlidge, John 72, 80, 89, 106, 135, 213

Zapotecs 120
zucchini *see* courgette

THE AUTHOR AND PHOTOGRAPHER

TOBY MUSGRAVE has a passion for horticulture and garden history which began at a very early age and shows no signs of abating. He has a degree in horticulture and a Ph.D in garden history, both from Reading University. An independent scholar since 1994, Toby has found an outlet for his enthusiasm and knowledge in a range of different media including books – this is his eighth, another is *The Head Gardeners* (2007) – television, radio, newspapers and magazines, as a lecturer, and most recently in a blog. Toby lives in Denmark, where his ¼-acre garden is an uneven mix of ornamentals, edibles and weeds, and where he finds the climate 'challenging'. For more information about Toby and his work, please visit www.TobyMusgrave.com

CLAY PERRY studied at Guildford School of Art, where he was a pupil of Ifor Thomas, a pioneer of photography as fine art, and went on to teach at Ravensbourne School of Art. His work, including portrait photography and reportage, has appeared in many publications, for instance *The Sunday Times, Country Living, World of Interiors* and *Homes & Gardens*. He has had exhibitions at the Special Photographer's Gallery, The Slaughter House Gallery, England and Co. and recently one on 'The Tribes of Morocco' at the Mediterranean Music Festival in Tangier. Numerous books featuring Clay's work have been published, including *English Country Gardens, The Glory of the English Garden, Vanishing Greece, David Austin's English Roses, Fantastic Flowers, Iris, Tulip* and *The Resilient Garden*.

ACKNOWLEDGMENTS

TOBY MUSGRAVE

IN MEMORIAM: I would like to dedicate this book to the memory of my best and life-long friend Nick Clamp, who loved life and his kitchen garden and who died too many decades too soon on 16 July 2009.

The creation of any book is a team effort and I should first like to say a big 'thank you' to Clay Perry. It has been a pleasure to work with Clay and his photographs are both beautiful and imaginative. Without these works of art this book would not be. This project has taken several years to come to fruition and I would like also to express my sincere thanks to those who have nurtured the book from its genesis and who have made its delivery positively pleasurable: at the Royal Horticultural Society Susannah Charlton, Rae Spencer-Jones, Simon Maughan and Guy Barter; and all the team at Thames & Husdon.

Especial thanks are extended to Grace Duke at the online Biodiversity Heritage Library (www. biodiversitylibrary.org) for her kindness and enthusiasm in dealing with my many requests and facilitating the scanning and uploading of so many primary source volumes to the BDH online catalogue. Without her help the process of research would have been far more time consuming and inconvenient.

I would like to thank the many people who are passionately concerned with the preservation of heritage and heirloom varieties on both sides of the Atlantic and who have generously and enthusiastically given of their time and expertise to answer questions and queries. In particular to George DeVault at Seed Savers Exchange and Thomas Etty Esq., whose catalogue is a masterpiece. Also, thanks to everyone who has helped source and supply the fruits and vegetables photographed, in particular Candy Smit and the garden staff at the Lost Gardens of Heligan.

Last, but by no means least, my heartfelt thanks as always to Vibeke. For your support in so many different ways, your patience and your always wise counsel. *Tusind tak skat.*

CLAY PERRY

There are so many people to thank for their help in this book. It has been a pleasure to work with Toby Musgrave, whose sense of history and knowledge of horticulture I greatly admire and whose feeling for the subject is reflected throughout these pages.

I would like to thank all the following: Candy Smit at the Lost Gardens of Heligan, without whose help and continuous support and encouragement this book would not have been possible; Nicola Bradley, head gardener at Heligan, for endless help supplying fruit and vegetables; Ruth Perkins, who together with Candy and Tim Smit, ferried mountains of produce on the train from Cornwall and kept me in constant supply of new things to photograph; Jim Arbury at the RHS gardens at Wisley and Sally Roger at the National Fruit Collection, Brogdale; Claire Bigwood and Rudy Bintein, gardeners at Thornage Hall, Norfolk, who are doing splendid work with biodynamics and heritage vegetables; Hamid and Sima Habibi at Keepers Nursery for their supply of apples, quince and medlars; the garden staff at Ham House for help with pictures, which we were unable to use for editorial reasons; Sarah Wayne and Jim Buckland at West Dean, also Celia Dickenson and Alex Miller for their help with tomatoes and chillis; Colin Randel at Thompson & Morgan for his assistance; and David Noble Jr for making the framing device which was so helpful in re-creating the Spanish atmosphere; also Paul Graham for his tireless help and assistance with the computer and things technical. And I second Toby's thanks to all at the RHS and Thames & Hudson.

Lastly I would like to thank my wife Maggie who has given me constant support while working on this book.